1940

Volume V 1950

Other Publications:
YOUR HOME
THE ENCHANTED WORLD
THE KODAK LIBRARY OF CREATIVE PHOTOGRAPHY
GREAT MEALS IN MINUTES
THE CIVIL WAR
PLANET EARTH
COLLECTOR'S LIBRARY OF THE CIVIL WAR
THE EPIC OF FLIGHT
THE GOOD COOK
THE SEAFARERS
WORLD WAR II
HOME REPAIR AND IMPROVEMENT
THE OLD WEST

For information on and a full description of any of the Time-Life Books series listed above, please write:
Reader Information
Time-Life Books
541 North Fairbanks Court
Chicago, Illinois 60611

This volume is one of a series
that chronicles American culture from 1870 to 1970.

This Fabulous Century V.5

1940 1950

Volume V

By the Editors of TIME-LIFE BOOKS

Time-Life Books, Alexandria, Virginia

Time-Life Books Inc.
is a wholly owned subsidiary of
TIME INCORPORATED

FOUNDER: Henry R. Luce 1898-1967

Editor-in-Chief: Henry Anatole Grunwald
President: J. Richard Munro
Chairman of the Board: Ralph P. Davidson
Corporate Editor: Jason McManus
Group Vice President, Books: Reginald K. Brack Jr.
Vice President, Books: George Artandi

TIME-LIFE BOOKS INC.

EDITOR: George Constable
Executive Editor: George Daniels
Editorial General Manager: Neal Goff
Director of Design: Louis Klein
Editorial Board: Dale M. Brown, Roberta Conlan,
Ellen Phillips, Gerry Schremp, Gerald Simons,
Rosalind Stubenberg, Kit van Tulleken, Henry Woodhead
Director of Research: Phyllis K. Wise
Director of Photography: John Conrad Weiser

PRESIDENT: William J. Henry
Senior Vice President: Christopher T. Linen
Vice Presidents: Stephen L. Bair, Robert A. Ellis,
John M. Fahey Jr., Juanita T. James, James L. Mercer,
Joanne A. Pello, Paul R. Stewart, Christian Strasser

THIS FABULOUS CENTURY

EDITOR: Ezra Bowen
Editorial Staff for *Volume V, 1940-1950*
Picture Editors: Mary Y. Steinbauer,
Carlotta Kerwin
Designer: John R. Martinez
Assistant Designer: Jean Lindsay Morein
Staff Writers: Tony Chiu, Sam Halper,
Anne Horan, Lucille Schulberg, Bryce S. Walker,
Edmund White, Peter Yerkes
Researchers: Alice Baker, Terry Drucker, Marcia A. Gillespie,
Helen Greenway, Lea Guyer, Helen M. Hinkle,
Carol Isenberg, Nancy J. Jacobsen,
Myra Mangan, Mary Kay Moran, Patricia Smalley,
Johanna Zacharias
Copy Coordinator: Susan B. Galloway
Design Assistant: Anne B. Landry
Picture Coordinator: Elizabeth A. Dagenhardt

EDITORIAL OPERATIONS
Design: Ellen Robling (assistant director)
Copy Room: Diane Ullius
Editorial Operations: Caroline A. Boubin (manager)
Production: Celia Beattie
Quality Control: James J. Cox (director), Sally Collins
Library: Louise D. Forstall

Correspondents: Elisabeth Kraemer-Singh (Bonn); Margot Hapgood, Dorothy Bacon (London); Miriam Hsia, Susan Jonas, Lucy T. Voulgaris (New York); Maria Vincenza Aloisi, Josephine du Brusle (Paris); Ann Natanson (Rome). Valuable assistance was also provided by: J. Patrick Barker (Oklahoma City), Jane Beatty (Philadelphia), Pam Burke (Los Angeles), Patricia Chandler (New Orleans), Juliane Greenwalt (Detroit), Blanche Hardin (Denver), Sandra Hinson (Orlando), Dick Hitt (Dallas), Joan Gerard Larkin (San Francisco), Frank Leeming Jr. (St. Louis), Holland McCombs (Dallas), Nancy McDonald (Montgomery), Frank Ney (Cedar Rapids), Richard Rawe (Cincinnati), Jane Rieker (Miami), William Roberts (Indianapolis), Gayle Rosenberg (Los Angeles), George Thurston (Tallahassee), Sue Wymelenberg (Boston).

Contents

America 1940 - 1950   6

    THE GATHERING STORM   21

Teenagers   26

    ACNE VS. THE A-BOMB   28

    DANCING TO THE TEEN STEP   36

    THE VOICE   47

Clubwomen   52

    A MEDDLE OF MATRONS   54

The War   64

    THE DAY THE CAT JUMPED   66

    Combat—The Island War   72

    WE YOU COMING-TO-GET, YANK   78

    The Sea War   80

    THE "BORIE'S" LAST BATTLE   86

    The Air War   88

    VIGIL AT A BOMBER BASE   92

    The Land War   94

    A TOUCH OF IKE   97

    A LOVELY DAY FOR A STROLL   100

    BADGES OF COURAGE   106

    OUR HEROES   108

    THE MOSTEST HERO   117

    At Ease   120

    NOTHING LIKE A DAME   122

    THE JOYS OF HOUSEKEEPING   127

    THE BITTER EDGE   136

Home Front   140

    THE TAXPAYERS' WAR   142

    The Industrial Muscle   146

    SOUR GRAPES FROM GERMANY   148

    A Common Cause   154

    SKY PILOTS   156

    VITAMINS FOR VICTORY   158

    THE GREATEST MOTHER   161

    GOING BY THE BOOK   164

The Call to Arms   168

    A GOOD WAC NEVER GETS PWOP   176

    BIG NIGHT WITH THE BROADS   178

    War Comes to Fantasyland   180

    THE FUNNIES FIGHT THE FASCISTS   183

    EVERYBOY   187

    BUGLE CALLS FROM TIN PAN ALLEY   189

    LIGHT LOOK AT A DARK TIME   190

    The Enemy Within   194

    A FLICKER OF THE WAR   197

    THE SUBMARINE CAPER   198

    NO JAPS WANTED   201

After the War   208

    THE READJUSTMENT   210

Sports   222

    THE END OF THE LONG WAIT   224

    A GALAXY OF GOOFBALLS   226

    BIG NOISE AT THE BALLPARK   228

    "IF YOU WERE ONLY WHITE"   230

    BOXING'S LIFE MASTERS   237

    GAUDY STAR OF THE ELECTRONIC SIDE SHOW   240

    FREEWHEELING BRAWL   242

Fashion   246

    THE DISTANT DRUM   248

    DIOR DECREES THE HIDDEN LEG   250

    THE NEW LOOK IN ARKANSAS   253

    A MILITARY NOTE   254

    SKIRTING REGULATIONS   256

    ACCENT ON ACCESSORIES   258

    FADS AND FANTASIES   260

    THE CROWNING TOUCH   262

Theater   264

    OH, WHAT A BEAUTIFUL ERA   266

    THE SOUR SMELL OF SUCCESS   268

    A SMILE GETS YOU NO PLACE   272

    THE RH FACTOR   274

TEXT CREDITS 284   PICTURE CREDITS 284   BIBLIOGRAPHY 285   ACKNOWLEDGMENTS 285   INDEX 286

The wedding of a young lieutenant in Montgomery, Alabama, 1944.

Tourists at a Cherokee Indian reservation in North Carolina, 1945.

A Missouri draft board hears out a hardship plea, 1942.

13

Summertime in Garden City, Long Island, 1942.

15

A milestone B-17 and its builders, Seattle, 1944.

Contestants for the title of fairest carhop in Galveston, Texas, 1941.

Picnickers from Ohio on the beach at Sarasota, Florida, 1940.

INNOCENCE ABROAD

The Gathering Storm

*I have said this before, but I shall say it again and again and again: Your boys are
not going to be sent into any foreign wars.*   FRANKLIN DELANO ROOSEVELT, OCTOBER 30, 1940

On New Year's Day of 1940, though Germany had clamped
an iron fist around Central Europe and Japan was rap-
ing China, most Americans were peaceably preoccupied
with their own homegrown affairs. They were lining up
at movie theaters to see the film version of *Gone With the
Wind,* Margaret Mitchell's romantic novel of the Old
South. They were betting on whether a nimble, bantamweight Tennessee eleven would trounce the brawny 220-
pounders of Southern California in the Rose Bowl. They
were feeding nickels into roadhouse jukeboxes to hear
Wee Bonnie Baker warble "Oh, Johnny! Oh!" And they
were looking ahead to the nation's quadrennial circus,
the Presidential conventions, where the biggest question
would be whether That Man in the White House, never a
stickler for tradition, would shatter yet another precedent
and run for a third term—a question on which the subject himself kept smilingly silent.

To many Americans, there seemed little else worth worrying about. True, some big trouble had been brewing
overseas. But U.S. citizens assured themselves that they
were "two broad oceans" away from foreigners' ancient
quarrels. The Japanese would never dare to bother America. China was what Japan wanted, and China was on
the other side of the globe. Besides, the European war
now appeared to be at a standstill. Four months had
passed since the Nazi dictator Adolf Hitler had sent his
Panzers into Poland—and by so doing embroiled himself
in war with those two bastions of democracy, Britain and
France. Since the quick destruction of Poland in September 1939 so little had happened that Idaho Senator
William E. Borah, a devout isolationist ever since World
War I, dubbed this one the "phony war." While the war
stood still, American sentiment remained where it had
been in the 1930s, when the U.S. Government had pledged
itself, by a series of neutrality acts, to remain aloof from
European entanglements. A poll conducted by Elmo Roper in December 1939 showed that 67.4 per cent of the
American people were opposed to taking sides.

But though most Americans might be babes in a wood
of cannon, as cartoonist Vaughan Shoemaker pictured
them *(opposite),* there were indications that some people
in the nation were growing up fast. Of nine major bills before Congress when it reconvened in January, five had to
do with the U.S. stance in the world at large. Two thirds
of the space in TIME magazine's major news departments
in the month of January was taken up by reports of the

events abroad. Beginning on January 13, *The New York Times* listed the highlights of foreign news in a front-page box called "The International Situation." And when President Roosevelt gave his State of the Union message, he began by alluding to foreign affairs, then asked Congress for $1.8 billion to finance the greatest peacetime military build-up in the entire history of the United States.

The first reaction of most people to Roosevelt's foresight was to be either skeptical or outraged. But, as spring came around, the situation in Europe suddenly worsened. In April Hitler's troops overran Denmark in a few hours, Norway in a matter of days. In May they stormed through Belgium, Luxembourg and the Netherlands. Next they crushed France—whose modernized army had been considered the best in the world. Italy, seeking a share in the spoils, entered the war on the side of Germany. F.D.R. intoned: "The hand that held the dagger has struck it into the back of its neighbor." The two strong fascist nations, calling themselves the Axis powers, ruthlessly set about seizing the rest of Europe.

As they did so, Americans faced some hard new facts of international life. Hitler now controlled all of Western Europe. Only Britain and the ocean stood between Germany and the U.S.—and the Atlantic did not look quite so broad or so reassuring any more, for Britain's ability to defend the seas was clearly in doubt. Hitler's submarines had sunk 75,000 tons of British shipping in May, and his surface navy was berthed in newly acquired French ports, preparing for an invasion of England. The effect of all this on American opinion showed up dramatically in a Roper poll conducted in May: now 67.5 per cent of the people favored giving active help to Britain —a complete about-face of majority opinion in a period of less than six months.

President Roosevelt officially marked the breach in U.S. neutrality. "We will extend to the opponents of force the material resources of this nation," he said. He asked Congress for another $4.8 billion to further beef up American armaments. He urged manufacturers to bring the production of planes up to 50,000 a year. "*Unglaublich!*

[Unbelievable!]" roared Field Marshal Hermann Goering, mastermind of German aviation. But Roosevelt knew his nation and its talents; the U.S. was soon producing planes at an average annual rate of 60,000.

Yet there still remained a third of a nation that thought the U.S. should take no sides—and this minority was a noisy one, with deep historical roots. A strong isolationist strain had existed in the American character ever since George Washington had enjoined his countrymen to "steer clear of permanent alliances with any portion of the foreign world." Those who felt that way in 1940-1941 were well organized, highly voluble and well entrenched on Capitol Hill, and they uttered shouts of "Interventionism!" over America's impulse to help the Allies.

Beginning in the summer of 1940, some 700 citizens' committees sprang up to debate the wisdom of what seemed to be a drift toward war. The majority were isolationist and most conspicuous was the America First Committee. In less than six months the America Firsters gathered 60,000 members—among them Alice Longworth, daughter of former President Teddy Roosevelt; Kathryn Lewis, daughter of labor leader John L.; and Colonel Charles A. Lindbergh, the Lone Eagle of 1927. "Let us stop this hysterical chatter of invasion," said Lindbergh, who had been well entertained in Berlin by Field Marshal Goering. "The three most important groups which have been pressing this country toward war are the British, the Jewish and the Roosevelt Administration."

"Warmonger" became a favorite isolationist epithet to be hurled at F.D.R. and his coterie. And in the summer of 1940, the Administration and a majority in Congress gave the critics a big new reason for using the word. At that time the U.S. Army ranked 17th in total manpower and modern weapons among the armies of the world —without even the capacity of the late Polish army, which Hitler's troops had squashed in 27 days. Clear-eyed citizens had no intention of allowing the United States to remain so feeble. And in June Senator Edward R. Burke and Representative James W. Wadsworth brought before Congress the Selective Training and Service Bill, which called for the first peacetime draft in the nation's history.

Isolationists inside of Congress and out were almost apoplectic. "If you pass this bill," thundered Montana Senator Burton K. Wheeler, "you accord Hitler his greatest and cheapest victory to date." Representative Martin L. Sweeney, an ardent Irishman and popular spokesman for his district in Cleveland, Ohio, called conscription a scheme to deliver the U.S. to the British devils. The conservative *Chicago Tribune*, of course, thundered against the draft. And in Los Angeles an outraged citizen declared, with more passion than clarity, that "conscription means both syphilis and slavery." However, a Gallup poll of mid-August indicated that in this time of fast-converging war clouds, the nation was 71 per cent behind the draft bill. The feeling in Congress was equally strong—so much so that supporters hardly bothered to argue for the bill. It became law on September 16.

Those who saw in the draft the demise of democratic practices took heart in another major event of the summer: that uniquely popular and disorderly American institution, the Presidential campaign. This year's contest was particularly absorbing. For in Washington That Man delighted his Democratic admirers—and confirmed the worst nightmares of conservative Republicans—by breaking the 144-year-old precedent against running for a third Presidential term. After remaining mysteriously silent throughout the preliminaries, in July he "allowed" himself to be "drafted" *in absentia* at the Democratic convention in Chicago. While he casually played solitaire by the White House radio, his managers artfully staged a demonstration that rocked the convention hall with "We Want Roosevelt!" Whereupon the President found he could not "decline to serve my country."

In Philadelphia, meanwhile, the Republican convention had come up with the dark horse of the century in Wendell Willkie, a tousle-headed, broad-grinning Hoosier and one-time Democrat who seemed to have a little something in him that appealed to everybody. Harold Ickes, Roosevelt's sardonic Secretary of the Interior, called him "the barefoot boy from Wall Street." Willkie had sprung full-blown into politics from a $75,000-a-year job as president of the Commonwealth and Southern Corporation, a large utilities firm. Yet he came wearing rumpled suits, adorned day after day with the same old tie, which gave him the air of a country bumpkin. He wore no watch and kept no car (he had never learned how to drive) and he amiably left the door to his Fifth Avenue apartment unlocked because that was what his father had done back home in Indiana. He called Roosevelt "the Champ" and said he was anxious to meet him. But the boyish demeanor concealed a powerful and cosmopolitan mind. Willkie had a scholarly bent; he read four books a week and could discourse as easily on Keynesian economics as on the feeding

HE'S NOT SAYING WHETHER HE WANTS TO HOOK IT OR NOT

habits of hogs. He was the most formidable opponent Roosevelt had faced in some 30 years of political life.

Ideologically, there was little difference between the platforms of the two candidates. On domestic issues Willkie was so close to Roosevelt that Norman Thomas, perennial Socialist candidate for President, said of him: "He agreed with Roosevelt's entire program of social reforms—and said it was leading to disaster." On foreign policy, both candidates favored aid to Britain.

Faced with the lack of a real issue, Republicans tried to create one out of Roosevelt's bid for a third term, and they peppered the campaign with shouts of "dynasticism" and "dictatorship." But with Europe a smoking ruin—and with the U.S. national income $40 billion above the point

to which it had sunk in the last Republican administration —the third-term issue seemed pretty small potatoes to most voters. When November came, a record 50 million Americans went to the polls. Over 22 million voted for the able and appealing Willkie—the largest total racked up by any Republican in the century. But 27 million others voted to keep Roosevelt where he was.

Once his campaign was over and his victory at the polls was certain, the President set about securing further aid for Britain, which was now in desperate straits. Since August 8th Germany had been raining bombs on British cities, in one night alone causing 1,500 fires to break out in London. The gallant and dogged Royal Air Force had extracted a deadly price from the German Luftwaffe, thus delaying Hitler's plans for invasion, but still the bombing continued. And it came with stunning reality right into American living rooms. In August CBS correspondent Edward R. Murrow had begun broadcasting live from London every evening. His sonorous "This . . . is London" was soon as familiar to Americans as the silvery tones of F.D.R.'s "My friends." Familiar, too, both as background on Murrow's broadcasts and on newsreel soundtracks, were the wail of air raid sirens, the scream of German bombs and the thunder of antiaircraft fire over London.

By late fall, there was a serious question as to how much longer Britain would be able to hold out. Apart from the loss of lives, planes and shipping, Britain's exchequer was almost totally depleted. Between the beginning of the war, in September 1939, and November 1940, the British Government had spent $4.5 billion for armaments in the United States alone; now it had less than $2 billion left in reserve. But Roosevelt came up with an ingenious plan to meet that dire circumstance. He called a news conference on December 17th and, after saying, "I don't think there is any particular news, except possibly one thing," he went on to discourse for 45 minutes on a concept that was in fact the biggest news since the Republican nomination of Wendell Willkie.

"Suppose my neighbor's house catches fire, and I have a length of garden hose," the President began. "If he can

Umbrella Road

take my garden hose and connect it up with his hydrant, I may help him to put out the fire.

"Now what do I do? I don't say to him before that operation, 'Neighbor, my garden hose cost me $15; you have to pay me $15 for it.' What is the transaction that goes on? I don't want $15—I want my garden hose back after the fire is over."

With that homily the President introduced what came to be known as the Lend-Lease bill, the boldest program yet conceived to aid the Allies. It provided for aid to "any country whose defense the President deems vital to the defense of the United States." The beneficiaries of Lend-Lease would not have to pay in cash; instead they would reciprocate with other goods and services. "What I am trying to do," the President said, "is to eliminate the silly, foolish dollar sign." In addition to this shocker for the isolationists, the bill contained another that was even worse for Roosevelt haters: It gave him powers that no previous President had ever had at his disposal. He could name any item he chose a defense article and designate any country he chose to receive it.

General Hugh Johnson, once head of Roosevelt's National Recovery Act but lately a defector from the Administration's ranks, roared that the Lend-Lease bill was "humanitarian lollipopping all over the world." Senator Wheeler, harking back to the old New Deal AAA farm program, under which farmers were paid for leaving land fallow, made a lengthy speech in which he called Lend-Lease a "Triple-A foreign policy: it will plough under every fourth American boy." An irritated colleague of Senator Wheeler's growled: "He talked long enough to let Hitler take another country." Representative Hamilton Fish of New York, another leading isolationist, cried that the bill would leave Congress "with no more authority than the German Reichstag." But the tide was running against the isolationists. Seventy per cent of Fish's constituents favored the bill he denounced. Wendell Willkie, supporting the man who had defeated him, observed that "it is the history of democracy that under such dire circumstances, extraordinary powers must be granted to the elected ex-

ecutive." Most Americans agreed, and the bill passed the House by a vote of 260 to 165, the Senate by 60 to 31. "This is really a fast piece of work for Washington," said the President; he immediately read it, asked a few questions and initialed it. It became law at 3:50 p.m. on March 11, and the next day Congress appropriated seven billion dollars to put it into effect.

Europe's reaction to the passage of the bill was instant and emphatic. Prime Minister Winston Churchill of Britain hailed it, describing it as the "Third Climacteric" of the war—the first two being the fall of France and the Battle of Britain—and his fellow Britons joyously flew American flags on the streets of London. The Italian press made the saber-rattling observation that "Roosevelt's gesture may cause many unpleasant surprises to England and the United States in the Pacific." Hitler said defiantly that Lend-Lease or no, "England will fall."

The significance of Lend-Lease began to make itself evident within a few months. Whereas the United States had managed to put together a grand total of 16 tanks in March 1941, by the end of the year, 951 tanks had been shipped to Britain. By Christmas of that year food shipments reached one million tons, while the overall output of trucks, planes, guns and ammunition was stepped up at a comparable pace. This effort, while filling the present needs of Britain, simultaneously stocked America's own arsenal against the future.

As many an America Firster had feared, Lend-Lease turned out to be a major prelude to much deeper American involvement in the war—but not in a way that anyone had been able to discern. The growing military power of the United States and the strengthening of its bond with Britain loomed as a mortal threat to one agressor nation that America was not watching with enough care. On the morning of December 7, 1941, hopes for peace went up in the smoke of Pearl Harbor *(page 66)*—and so did the last vestiges of isolationism. "The only thing to do now," said Senator Wheeler in an about-face, as he joined with the rest of the Congress to declare war—not only on Tokyo but on Berlin and Rome as well—"is to lick hell out of them."

Bobbysoxers attain high fashion by mismatching shoes and socks.

Acne vs. the A-Bomb

Few young people share deeply in the life of a group dedicated, and actively devoted, to the highest goals of mankind. SOCIAL SCIENTIST MURRAY G. ROSS, 1950

I think you should have more articles on dates and shyness and put in some more about movie stars, too. Stories like those on atomic energy are very boring.
LETTER TO THE EDITOR OF *SEVENTEEN* MAGAZINE, 1946

Once upon a time the awkward, gangling Americans living in the penumbra between grammar school and a job were deplored as creatures called adolescents. But by the mid-'40s, a notable change had occurred in the status of the adolescent. Suddenly, he emerged with the brand-new —and far more respectable—label of teenager. Adolescence evolved into a cult, to be prolonged, enjoyed, and commercially catered to as never before.

No one will ever know for sure how or why this change occurred. Clearly, though, the war played a major role. With everyone over 18 in the service, younger boys were often the biggest men in town. And for the first time since the Depression, they had money in their pockets, picked up in the many jobs available in the scarce labor market. Girls, too, earned spending money in a new profession: baby-sitting for parents on night shifts at war plants.

The teen-age phenomenon was quickly spotted—and boosted—by a variety of shrewd merchandisers. Among the first to cash in on the teen market were song writers and the manufacturers of phonographic equipment *(pages 36-37)*. In the strictly female market, Minx Modes, one of the healthiest members of a family of booming junior-fashions manufacturers, sold $12 million worth of frocks be-

tween 1944 and 1946. In the former year appeared *Seventeen,* a magazine solely devoted to the fashions, foibles and problems of young girls. Stadium Girl lipstick and other make-up blossomed on thousands of high-school faces; the Chicago *Daily News* started a wildly popular column of teen-age news titled Keen Teens; in 1949 the august *Ladies' Home Journal* inaugurated a new section called Profile of Youth; and all across the nation teen-age canteens became prime watering holes for jitterbugs and milk-shake drinkers on weekend evenings.

Throughout this early stage of the teen-age revolution, the kids themselves remained responsive to traditional parental discipline, became almost compulsively conformist within their own age group, and were massively unconcerned with world problems. A survey carried out by Purdue University to define the major concerns of teenagers in the '40s revealed that 33 per cent felt there was nothing they, personally, could or should do to prevent wars; 50 per cent of all girls regarded their own figures as their No. 1 preoccupation; 37 per cent of all boys were primarily concerned with having "a good build"; and one third of all those 2,000 questioned agreed that the most serious problem facing the American teenager was acne.

Card sharks relax in the privacy of a buddy's place. Walls festooned with filched signs and Petty girls were de rigueur for teen-age boys' rooms.

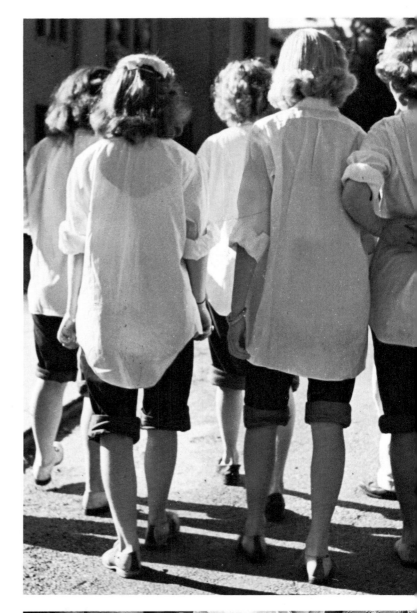

The overwhelming urge of the teenager of the '40s was to be like every other teenager. Girls, especially, looked like peas in a disheveled pod—and the pod was often borrowed from the males. Though the girls never went so far as to wear the Army boots *(upper right)* affected by hordes of schoolboys, they did appear in baggy, rolled-up blue jeans and sloppy shirttails, and even striped football socks. On dates, however, the youngsters took care to be appropriately feminine. In pursuit of this goal the girls devoured all kinds of advice from magazines, newspapers and books *(excerpted below)* on how to do the Right Thing—i.e., hold the interest of the notoriously distractible young male.

The moment with the family may be a bad one . . . but the next moment, when you are alone with Jimmy for the first time, may hold even greater terrors. What are you going to talk about? Bravely you start something: "Gee . . . it's hot tonight, isn't it?" Your voice trails—and dies. You've had your say. And one that requires nothing more than "Yes" or "No" from Jimmy. Which is no way to start a conversation. Jimmy may be just as shy as you are. His heart is thumping . . . his thoughts running round and round—just like yours. A smart Teen-Ager thinks about how to start a conversation with Jimmy long before she closes the front door behind her. This does not mean planned sentences —copying Susie's line, popping out with the newest slang phrase every other minute. It means figuring out subjects of mutual interest that make good conversation easy. Look over these conversation starters:

■ *Tell Jimmy you remember the first time you ever laid eyes on him: "It was the first day of school three years ago in Latin class and you were wearing a red tie."*

■ *Talk about animals. "My dog has fleas—what'll I do?"*

■ *Talk about foreign languages: "Are you taking French?" "Have you ever traveled?"* — EDITH HEAL, *TEEN-AGE MANUAL,* 1948

All-Girl, All-Night Show

*During the '40s, a regular Friday-night ceremony was an all-girl sleep-in
called a slumber party. In 1943 "Life" magazine dispatched a photographer and a reporter
to reconstruct for its 22 million readers the antics of a clutch of Midwestern kids
as they bedded down for some soul-soothing female chatter. The results are shown here.*

 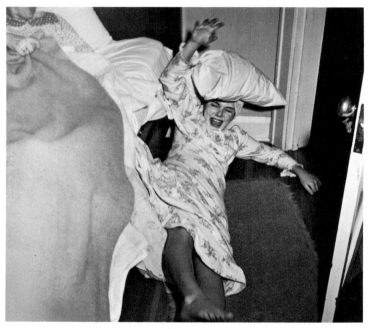

 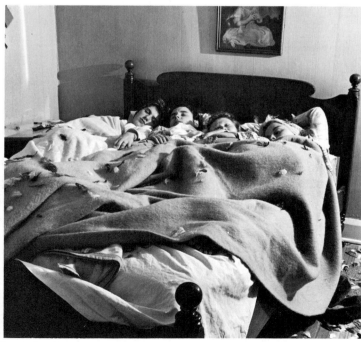

Indianapolis girls warm up for a slumber party with a rambunctious pillow fight, then squirm and squeeze four in a bed for an attempt at sleep.

Ready for a frolic, a pretty teenager from Webster Groves, Missouri, makes her entrance in rag hair-curlers and her father's oversized pajamas.

Not Many Rebels

*Though parents, as always, saw their
teenagers as flagrant nonconformists, most kids
lived and dressed (below) by rigid codes.*

Regulation gear included sloppy trousers, loafers and dangling shirttails.

Preparing for a coed picnic, fraternity boys at a Kansas college toss blankets

Fads like the broad, baggy "zoot suit" won brief approval, but soon died, the victims of teenage conventionalism.

into a jalopy. Such rituals were held at the same time year after year.

This shopper shyly appraised a zoot suit, then rejected it as too extreme.

OH! LOOK AT ME NOW!
Featured by Tommy Dorsey and His Orchestra

A NIGHTINGALE SANG IN BERKELEY SQUARE
(BARKLEY)
by Eric Maschwitz and Manning Sherwin

MAIRZY DOATS

I'LL WALK ALONE
Lyric by SAMMY CAHN
Music by JULE STYNE

ELMER'S TUNE
by ELMER ALBRECHT · SAMMY GALLOP · DICK JURGENS

I HEAR A RHAPSODY
By GEORGE FRAGOS
JACK BAKER and
DICK GASPARRE

RUM and Coca-Cola
Lyric by MOREY AMSTERDAM
Music by JERI SULLAVAN and PAUL BARON
Featured by ANDREWS SISTERS with VIC SCHOEN and his Orchestra

GREEN EYES
(AQUELLOS OJOS VERDES)
Canción Bolero
SPANISH LYRIC BY ADOLFO UTRERA
MUSIC BY NILO MENENDEZ

ON A SLOW BOAT TO CHINA
FRANK LOESSER
A Frank Loesser Song
FEATURED BY JIMMY DORSEY AND HIS ORCHESTRA WITH HELEN O'CONNELL AND BOB EBERLY

ONE DOZEN ROSES

1619 BROADWAY, New York City, N. Y.

Juke Box Saturday Night

Moppin' up soda pop rickeys
To our heart's delight
Dancin' to swingeroo quickies
Juke box Saturday night

Money, we really don't need that
We make out all right,
Lettin' the other guy feed that
Juke box Saturday night

Dancing to the Teen Step

Saturday nights, swarms of teenagers shuttled between the soda shop with the best-stocked jukebox and the home of whoever was throwing the best open house *(right)*. Along with their herd instinct and the unending search for the opposite sex, these teenagers were migrating toward dance music like the hit numbers shown above. This pursuit, besides being fun for the kids, produced an explosive growth in profits for the music industry, which delightedly geared up to please a fast-rising teen market. By 1946 record companies were selling 10 times as many songs as they had a decade earlier; that year RCA Victor and Decca sold 100 million records each. Two years later the industry got another boost when tough plastic 45-rpm and long-playing 33-rpm records made obsolete the brittle old 78-rpm stand-bys. The jukebox industry blossomed into an $80-million, 400,000-box business that consumed the astounding total of five billion nickels yearly. So deeply did the coin machines ingrain themselves in the national culture that the class gift of the 1947 graduates of Scarborough High School in New York was a jukebox.

Partygoers in Porterville, California, do a fast lindy. To sell teenagers their records, RCA in 1950 gave away $10 in 45 rpm's with every $40 player.

Messing Around

*Saturdays were a challenge that each teenager met in his own way—as long
as there was plenty of company. The football hero was cheered and fussed over (right); the
fraternity initiate went on his perilous rounds; but most kids indulged in
companionable time-killing, inelegantly but accurately known as "messing around."*

Listening to some records (but rarely buying) at Lemcke's in Webster Groves, Missouri

Pep rally before the game

Smooching at the open-house party

A scarf for the big man on campus

Having a soda at The Nook

Sneaking through a window for an initiation stunt

Teenagers

A dance at the gym

Making time with the date

A hot time at a beach party

Teenaging around with the boys

Knitting Argyles for fellows

Wearing the boyfriend's parka

With the gang at the roller rink

The Molesters Club operates on the Tin Lizzie

Perched on a convertible, Atlanta high-school kids gobble hamburgers after a game. Meeting at drive-ins was called "frogging" by Southern teenagers.

The Idols of the Young

*Seeking an insight into the values of modern youth, "Life" magazine in 1950 invited teenagers across the
country to list the individual they admired most. The result was the dozen heroes below.
Interpreting these choices, one college professor approved the idealizing of "muscle, brawn and brain,"
but found the admiration of "movie and radio people possibly a less reassuring trend."*

TOP ROW: AUTHOR LOUISA MAY ALCOTT, BASEBALL PLAYER JOE DI MAGGIO AND SONG-AND-DANCE GIRL VERA-ELLEN. BOTTOM ROW: PRESIDENTS FRANKLIN D. ROOSEVELT AND ABRAHAM LINCOLN AND MOVIE COWPOKE ROY ROGERS.

TOP ROW: ARMY GENERAL DOUGLAS MACARTHUR, RED CROSS FOUNDER CLARA BARTON AND ACTRESS-SINGER DORIS DAY. BOTTOM ROW: SISTER ELIZABETH KENNY, BASEBALL HOME RUN HITTER BABE RUTH AND NURSE FLORENCE NIGHTINGALE.

Frank Sinatra aims a hungry gaze at the audience as he slides through a lyric. His sultry style earned him well over one million dollars per year.

The Voice

On the morning of October 12, 1944—Columbus Day in the third grim year of World War II—a frail-looking youth with rumpled brown hair stepped onto the stage of the Paramount Theater in New York City. Expectant squeals broke from the 3,600 teen-age girls who had packed the house. Then, as the youth started singing, his blue eyes searching hungrily among the faces in front of him, his voice tender and silky, the audience exploded. Adolescent voices screamed in genuine ecstasy at each slowly modulated musical phrase. Scores of schoolgirls swooned from their seats at each golden note, and ushers with smelling salts and stretchers hastened to revive them.

Outside, in Times Square, the commotion was even greater. Some 10,000 frenzied bobbysoxers had laid siege to the Paramount box office. Twenty thousand others clogged the square, blocking traffic, trampling bystanders and crashing through store windows. An emergency contingent of more than 700 riot police, including 200 patrolmen transferred from the Columbus Day Parade, was hastily called in to restore order.

The cause of all this ruckus was Francis Albert Sinatra, a crooner of romantic ballads whose voice reminded one critic of worn velveteen and another of the cry of a love-sick loon. Known variously as The King of Swoon, Frank Swoonatra, The Voice That Thrills Millions, or simply The Voice, he was a totally new phenomenon. No other entertainer, not even Rudy Vallee or good old Bing Crosby, had ever inspired such wild adulation, such total surrendering collapse. According to one listener, it was as though Frankie had musk glands instead of vocal cords.

Adults were mystified. "As a visible male object of adulation, Sinatra is baffling," *Newsweek* confessed. And at a time when the accepted image of American manliness was a brawny soldier in combat fatigues, Sinatra indeed seemed an unlikely idol. At five feet ten and 135 pounds, the young singer seemed on the verge of collapse from malnutrition; the big gag in show biz was that you could not tell which was Sinatra and which was the microphone. Frankie's clothes only accentuated his general scrawniness. For daytime performances he wore enormous, high-waisted slacks, flashy sport jackets with immense padded shoulders and outsized bow ties that flopped like spaniels' ears. Said trumpeter Harry James, one of his early employers, "He looks like a wet rag."

Even Frankie's singing failed to convince some skeptics. "The swooner-crooner who makes every song sound just like every other song," sneered LIFE, could render in only one lugubrious tempo: "largo alla marcia funebre." Another critic complained that listening to Sinatra was like "being stroked by a hand covered with cold cream." But most of his fellow musicians were as enthusiastic as the bobbysoxers. "Call it talent," said torch singer Jo Stafford. "You knew he couldn't do a number badly."

Obviously it was more than Sinatra's well-tuned ear and evocative phrasing that galvanized the bobbysoxers. "Personally, I think it's on account of his personality," one young lady declared flatly. Various psychiatrists analyzed it differently: "mass hypnotism," "mass frustrated love," "mammary hyperesthesia," and, referring to Sinatra's wispy build, a maternal "urge to feed the hungry." Several commentators pointed out, with a modicum of cruel accuracy, that, with most young men in the army, Frankie was the only male around.

Sinatra himself had a simple explanation. "I'm twenty-five. I look maybe nineteen," he said. "Most of the kids feel like I'm one of them—the pal next door, say. So maybe they feel they know me. And that's the way I want it to be. What the hell, they're nice kids." And Sinatra did in fact seem to be a teenager himself—so vulnerable, so shy, so sincere, so terribly innocent.

But The Voice That Thrills Millions was, in reality, about as frail and innocent as an Army Ranger. He was born on December 12, 1915, in a cold-water tenement in the rugged waterfront section of Hoboken, New Jersey. From his father, a Sicilian immigrant who at one time made his way as a bantamweight prizefighter, Sinatra gained a taste for bare-knuckle brawling. From his strong-minded mother, who was active in local politics, he inherited a king-sized ambition and a quicksilver temper. By the time he had dropped out of high school, in the middle of his sophomore year, the skinny Sinatra had fought his way to leadership of a local gang of toughs. Crafty and cocky, he was dubbed "Angles" by his friends.

In 1933, at age 17, Frankie hit upon the Big Angle. He happened to buy tickets to a Bing Crosby concert at a local movie house, and became utterly entranced, both by Crosby's voice and his power over the public. "I can do that!" he exclaimed to his date, childhood sweetheart Nancy Barbato. Nancy, who loved him so much that she eventually married him, agreed.

The next seven years were a rough uphill battle for recognition. He sang at lodge meetings, entered amateur contests, filled in at local radio stations (his fee was 70 cents for carfare). In 1939, while he was singing at a small Jersey roadhouse, he was discovered and signed by Harry James, who was just starting his own band. Six months later, Frankie moved up to a spot with Tommy Dorsey, who was then one of the nation's top bandleaders. Over

---

I can sing that son of a bitch off the stage any day of the week.
SINATRA ON ANY RIVAL, 1945

---

the next two years with Dorsey, he was a screaming success in club dates, cut a basketful of hit records including "Fools Rush In," "White Christmas" and "Night and Day," and was on his way to becoming a national celebrity.

In the winter of 1942, Sinatra set out on his own. He bought out his contract with Dorsey, hired a press agent, and on December 30, 1942, opened the first of his notoriously successful engagements at the Paramount. A girl in the audience (who reportedly had not eaten lunch) swooned during the performance. Another girl squealed, and bedlam ensued. From then on, he was The Voice.

The epidemic of Sinatritis swept like measles through the nation's teenagers. Two thousand fan clubs sprang up, and the singer's fan mail rose to 5,000 letters a week. To get an autograph, frantic bobbysoxers would lie in wait in Frankie's dressing room or pursue him to nightclubs, restaurants and even to his home, where they would peek through the windows and try to climb into his bedroom. When it snowed, some of them lovingly dug up his

footprints and preserved them in the refrigerator. Others tried to tear off Frankie's clothes, and twice the singer barely escaped strangulation when two girls staged a frenetic tug of war with his bow tie. Even a few older women succumbed; one adult admirer approached him in the Waldorf hotel in 1943, ripped open her bodice and demanded he autograph her bra.

Frankie thrived on such hazards of success. "I'm riding high, kid," he told one reporter. And indeed he was. Within months of his Paramount debut, The Voice had hooked into a gilt-edged contract with Columbia Records to turn out his songs, signed to appear each week on *Your Hit Parade* and contracted with RKO to make a movie a year. His income leaped to a million dollars annually, and he moved to Hollywood, where he built a pink house that had a $7,000 machine just to close the curtains on one wall. Always impulsively generous with friends, he began passing out $150 gold cigarette lighters as though they were Baby Ruths.

Meanwhile the reaction of American adults ranged from mystification to outrage. "We can't tolerate young people making a public display of losing control of their emotions," proclaimed a New York City education commissioner, George Chatfield. The commissioner then threatened to press charges against Sinatra for encouraging truancy since thousands of girls were skipping school to hear him sing. In Congress, according to the *New York Herald Tribune*, it was stoutly affirmed that "The Lone Ranger and Frank Sinatra are the prime instigators of juvenile delinquency in America." In Hollywood the formidable columnist Elsa Maxwell charged the singer with "musical illiteracy" and further recommended that Frankie's fans be given "Sinatraceptives."

Much of the adult dislike of Frank Sinatra stemmed from an odd sort of affronted patriotism. Somehow it seemed unfair, while thousands of brave American lads were giving their lives on foreign beachheads, for a pint-sized entertainer back home to be earning millions of dollars as well as the adoration of the country's teen-age girls. "Is there no way to make those kids come to their senses?" asked a refugee from a German concentration camp, herself 17 years old. "The time they are wasting outside the Paramount Theater could be used for other purposes—for instance, to help win this war."

And it was true that Sinatra himself made little contribution to the war effort, though the failure to do so was not altogether his fault. He was called up on several occasions to take an Army physical exam—while tearful bobbysoxers mobbed the induction center—but he was classified 4-F because of a punctured eardrum. He did make one USO tour of Italy in 1945, shortly after V-E Day. And on returning home, he evoked the wrath of both soldiers and civilians by charging that the USO program was run by "shoemakers in uniform." "Mice make women faint, too," snidely observed the Army newspaper *Stars and Stripes*, and Marlene Dietrich, who had sung to frontline troops while enemy shells were bursting overhead, remarked that "you could hardly expect the European Theater to be like the Paramount."

Adult distaste for Frankie hung on past V-J Day. Ironically, it assaulted him even when he did something courageous and right. Sinatra had always possessed an instinctive urge to do battle for the underdog and had once impulsively slugged a counterman at a restaurant for refusing to serve a Negro. In 1945 he launched his own national campaign to stamp out racial prejudice. He preached tolerance on radio shows, to theater audiences and in high school auditoriums across the country. In 1946 he won a special Academy Award for a movie short on racial intolerance called *The House I Live In*.

Many Sinatraphobes had a hard time taking Frankie's crusading seriously. Others took outright offense. His tolerance campaign drew a barrage of fire from various right-wingers. The conservative Hearst newspaper chain hinted that Frankie was a Communist and in 1947 ran unsubstantiated stories that he was up for investigation by the House Committee on Un-American Activities.

Most of the hate-Sinatra barrage was similar, irresponsible hip-shooting. But something close to a bull's-eye came in February 1947 from Scripps-Howard columnist Robert Ruark, who at the time was following up a lead on the recently exiled Mafia boss, "Lucky" Luciano. Ruark had tracked Luciano to earth in Havana, where he found the racket czar surrounded by henchmen and apparently carrying on business much as usual. But whom should Ruark spot among the goons and bodyguards, consorting with America's most sinister crook, but—horror of horrors —Frank Sinatra, America's teen dream! "This curious desire to cavort among the scum is possibly permissible

---

Nobody comes before my wife Nancy. That goes for now and for all time.   SINATRA ON MATRIMONY, 1943

---

among citizens who are not peddling sermons to the nation's youth," admonished Ruark. "But Mr. Sinatra, the self-confessed savior of the country's small fry, seems to be setting a most peculiar example to his hordes of pimply, shrieking slaves."

The Voice fought back, verbally at first. "Any report that I fraternized with goons or racketeers is a vicious lie," he protested. But Frankie's gut response to such criticism was to use his fists. In April, while dining with friends at a fancy Hollywood restaurant, Sinatra spotted one of his loudest detractors, New York *Daily Mirror* writer Lee Mortimer, in a nearby booth. The way Mortimer told it, he got up to leave when suddenly he was jumped from behind by Sinatra and three thugs. The attack, said Mortimer, was a totally unprovoked surprise.

Frankie's version was notably different. "He gave me a look," the singer said. "He called me a dago son of a bitch, and I saw red." No one really knows who said what, but Sinatra ended up by paying Mortimer $9,000 in damages, admitting, "We all have our human weaknesses."

Other flaws began to show in the bobbysoxers' idol. For years Frankie had been billed as Hollywood's ideal husband. Now, showing a distinct taste for high-priced cheesecake, he deserted his wife Nancy and his three children. After a round of purported infidelities with various starlets, in February 1950 the singer was spotted dining tête-à-tête with Ava Gardner, then Hollywood's reigning

femme fatale. When a news photographer tried to film the couple, Sinatra threatened to break his nose.

There followed a tumultuous public courtship. With the press gleefully dogging his heels, the thoroughly smitten Frankie chased Ava back to Hollywood, to New York, to Spain (where the actress made a movie, and had an extracurricular fling with a bullfighter) and home again. The newspapers published each spicy detail: where the couple shared hotel rooms, where they did not; whether Frank gave Ava a $10,000 emerald necklace ("The only present I ever gave Ava was six bottles of coke," Frank sourly grunted) or whether he did not; whether Sinatra would divorce his wife or whether Nancy would divorce him.

Through it all, a hostile press reported Sinatra's ever more violent temper fits and moods of deep depression. Not only was Frankie making a stupendous spectacle of himself, the impulsive brawler was falling apart under the impact of Ava, who was dubbed the "Avalanche" and who had already left two husbands shattered and wan.

Sinatra's life was disintegrating in other sectors as well. A movie he made during 1948, *Miracle of the Bells,* clanged hollowly at the box office. Sales of his records were slipping alarmingly, and in 1949 he was dropped from his spot on *Your Hit Parade.* Teen-age swooners began drifting away in disillusioned armies to listen to Frankie Laine, Perry Como and Billy Eckstine. To cap it off, Sinatra's silken vocal cords were beginning to fray from overuse. At a nightclub engagement in New York in 1950, he suffered a massive throat hemorrhage. It seemed The Voice was silenced for good.

"Is the frenzied, swooning bobby-soxer disappearing from the U.S. scene?" the New York *Star* had asked as early as 1948. Even Frankie had to admit that the party seemed to be over. "From what I can determine there's a definite trend among the bobby-soxers. They're growing up," he said. His voice gone, his fans departed, it seemed Sinatra was finished. Perhaps there would be another road back to the top for the welterweight scrapper from Hoboken. But at the decade's end, there was every sign that Frankie, himself, might be going into his last swoon.

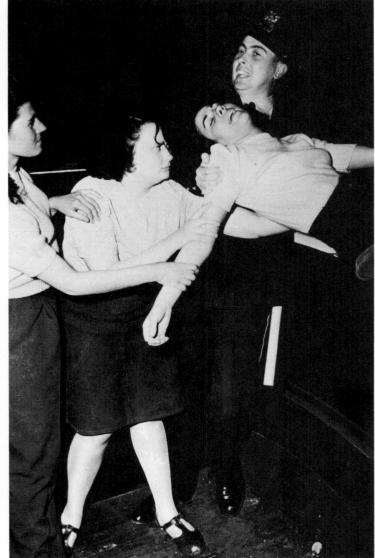

Wherever Frankie appeared, he was greeted by the wild adoration of what one critic called "imbecilic, moronic, screaming-meemie autograph kids."

Clubwomen

Accepting flowers, a club member announces, "My heart is too full."

A Meddle of Matrons

This plump crusader for tiny causes, this domestic robin pecking courageously at the boundless pastures of culture has a highly developed enough sense of civic duty to hope that a sale of her home-made gingerbread may save Tibet.   ALISTAIR COOKE, 1949

A ubiquitous and powerful figure on the American scene in the '40s was the clubwoman, devouring culture and cake, fighting Communism and overweight, preserving historical monuments, sponsoring child welfare and playing a great deal of bridge. The Bureau of Labor Statistics reported in 1947 that nearly half of the adult female population of the United States was idle; nearly 20 million women over 40 didn't work, had no children under 18 and yet were neither aged nor infirm. They made up a restless, indefatigable army of ladies who whiled away their days and nights serving on committees and discussing peaceful uses of the atom.

The gentle satirist who best captured the foibles of clubwomen was Helen Hokinson, a cartoonist for *The New Yorker*. Although she herself was a spinster and notably shy, she had a perfect eye and ear for catching her subjects at characteristic moments. A Hokinson matron asks a salesman in a bookstore: "Isn't it about time another one of John Gunther's 'Insides' came out?" At the beauty parlor she tells her hairdresser: "Now please bear in mind that I am not Ingrid Bergman." Madam President announces: "The Garden Committee reports that Mrs. Bernard Thayer, Mrs. Harrison S. Quigley,

and Mrs. Thompkins Sperry have all seen pussy willows."

Not everyone responded to the clubwoman as affectionately as Helen Hokinson. In 1947 Senator Robert A. Taft lashed out against the Federated Women's Clubs for being "utterly intolerant of any point of view which criticizes the policies endorsed by their national officers." Writer Philip Wylie was even more caustic. He claimed that the clubwoman had "not enough sex appeal to budge a hermit 10 paces off a rock ledge" and that she played bridge "with the stupid voracity of a hammerhead shark."

Despite such blasts, the clubwoman actually was trying to do her earnest best in behalf of a host of worthy activities, as shown by the pictures on the following pages of the Woman's Club of Chevy Chase, Maryland. British anthropologist Geoffrey Gorer might well have been thinking of these very ladies when he wrote in his book *American People:* "It is easy enough to laugh at these middle-aged women with their naive approach to the arts and to 'gracious living' (a key phrase). It hurts our dignity to think that our future is being determined by Helen Hokinson's grotesques, by the women with monotonous, insistent voices, who are dissatisfied with their bathrooms, by Madam Chairman. But one might easily be in worse hands."

"*But why don't you become a Democrat and _enjoy_ politics?*"

Ladies listen raptly as a speaker tells them: "Women's clubs can help in steering the world away from war; my solution is—world government."

Saving the World

During a 1946 meeting, the Woman's Club of Chevy Chase, Maryland, faces up squarely to its duty to help President Truman and the United Nations remake the postwar world.

A dissenter protests one-world government—but favors atoms for peace.

Seeking a Richer Life

To make sure that every spare hour was filled with useful activity,
most of the Chevy Chase Club's 800 members were enrolled in at least one enriching
study course. The most popular were singing, creative art, handicraft
and foreign language—all certain to lead to self-improvement and a fuller life.

Admiring one another's costumes, each from a different Latin country, the ladies immerse themselves in their own south-of-the-border fiesta.

A matron watches her mother make jewelry in the club's workshop.

The art section's second assistant chairman displays one of her works.

During the club's once-a-week Spanish class, shiny-eyed members listen as Señor Cromayer explains one of the complexities of his language.

The Tea Ceremony

*Bedecked in their newest hats, the ladies turned out for a tea party
in honor of Mrs. Harry Truman. Unfortunately, Mrs. Truman didn't make it, but
everyone agreed the pouring was a great success and special credit went
to the surplus cupcake committee for efficiently disposing of the leftover goodies.*

Beaming with all of the pride of a successful executive, a lady offers other members a tray of mixed canapés lovingly assembled by her committee.

Pouring, the most prestigious activity at any ladies' tea party, is handled with dignity and aplomb by a respected past president of the club.

"Miss Whitehead has come to tell us how to amuse sailors."

Marines swarm over a Japanese bunker on Tarawa.

The Day the Cat Jumped

Everything was ready. From Rangoon to Honolulu every man was at battle stations.

TIME MAGAZINE, LAST ISSUE BEFORE PEARL HARBOR

I don't know how the hell we were caught so unprepared.

JOE MARTIN, HOUSE REPUBLICAN LEADER, DECEMBER 8, 1941

Never in American history was an event more anticipated yet more of a surprise than the attack on Pearl Harbor. The tactics of a sneak raid on Pearl—crippling the formidable U.S. fleet based there and freeing the Japanese Navy to dominate the Pacific—had been a standard part of both Tokyo's and Washington's strategic thinking for a decade. From 1931 on, every graduating class at Japan's naval academy had faced the same final exam question: "How would you carry out a surprise attack on Pearl Harbor?" In 1932 a U.S. carrier showed how: sneaking in northeast of the island of Oahu in a pre-dawn "raid," its planes "sank" all the vessels at Pearl. Japanese observers reported the feat; Tokyo carefully recorded it.

In mid-1941, the theoretical danger to Pearl became very real. The long-standing rivalry between Japan and the U.S. for Pacific supremacy, bitterly sharpened by Japan's rape of China, was further aggravated by announced plans for broad expansion of Nippon's Greater East Asia Co-Prosperity Sphere. In effect this meant that all white devils were going to be kicked out of Asia. To check the Japanese momentum, the U.S. had already embargoed American oil and scrap metals—both vital to Japan's war machine. Then, in July, President Roosevelt brought mat-

ters to a head by freezing all Japanese assets in the U.S.

At the Imperial Palace in Tokyo, the militarists said there was now no alternative but war—and soon. Strike, they argued, before the U.S. embargo so weakened Japan and Roosevelt's push toward rearmament so strengthened the U.S. that the moment would be lost. With Emperor Hirohito's cautious help Japan's peacefully inclined civilian leaders won a compromise: the diplomats would get until November 29 to try for an accommodation with Washington; failing that, war.

A race began: talks in Washington, war preparations in Japan. In Washington, Japan's prime peace-talker was bumbling, kindly, 62-year-old Ambassador Kichisaburo Nomura. Given to hearty belly laughs and good whiskey, Nomura was an old Potomac hand; as naval attaché in Washington during World War I, he had worked with Assistant Secretary of the Navy Franklin D. Roosevelt. F.D.R. now welcomed "my old personal friend" to the White House for nine separate, chummy talks; and Tokyo's civilian chiefs allowed themselves a flicker of hope. To join the talks later came Special Envoy Saburo Kurusu, no old Presidential pal but a smooth diplomat with an American wife. Almost daily Nomura chattered away

Envoys Kurusu (left) and Nomura leave the State Department after a peace conference with Secretary Hull just 17 days before Pearl Harbor.

in his mournful singsong and horrid accent to U.S. Secretary of State Cordell Hull, who answered "that old codger" in a Tennessee drawl aggravated by ill-fitting dentures, so that neither fully understood the other.

Meanwhile, 13,000 miles away, 43 assorted admirals and captains in Japan's Navy War College schemed out the fleet plan for air attack on Pearl Harbor and decided it was feasible. Now, with Emperor Hirohito looking on anxiously, an elite group of hawks and doves secretly argued Japan's decision between peace and war.

The Emperor was not the only one watching. By a stroke of fortune so great that it was code-named "Magic," another small group of leaders—American leaders—were privy to Japan's agonized appraisal. Late in 1940 the Signal Corps had cracked "Purple," Japan's top diplomatic code, and after January 23, 1941, nine high U.S. government officials called "Ultras," among them President Roosevelt, were able every day to read the most secret communications between Tokyo and its diplomats.

"Magic" showed the Japanese doves growing increasingly downhearted about the negotiations. On October 16, Japan's civilian Premier, having barely escaped assassination by war hawks the month before and fearful that the next attempt would succeed, resigned with his cabinet; and General Hideki Tojo, a fire-eater, took over as Premier. Now the military was in the saddle. In Washington, the fascinated "Ultras"—via "Magic"—watched the danger draw closer and closer. November 4, 1941, Tokyo to Ambassador Nomura: "Relations between Japan and the U.S. have reached the edge. This is our last effort." November 22: "We will wait until Nov. 29. After that things are automatically going to happen."

But peace had already lost the race. On November 26, six radio-silenced Japanese carriers stole out of the remote Kuriles north of Japan, headed toward Pearl along the untraveled northern route. As the quiet, 32-ship fleet steamed in two parallel columns, another message flashed from Tokyo to Washington, November 28: "In two or three days negotiations will be de facto ruptured." Should Nomura yet perform a miracle in Washington, the attack

force could be recalled up to December 5. Else, the radio signal "Climb Mt. Niitaka" would send 353 carrier planes at dawn December 7 to blast the fleet at Pearl.

Pearl was in peril, but then almost every American war chief was supposed to have known it. On January 24, 1940, Navy Secretary Frank Knox wrote to Secretary of War Henry Stimson, "Hostilities would be initiated by a surprise attack on Pearl Harbor." In April 1941, joint estimates by the commanders of the Army and Navy air forces defending Pearl concluded that Japan "can probably employ a maximum of six carriers which would probably approach inside of 300 miles. A dawn air attack might be a complete surprise." The Pacific Fleet commander himself, Rear Admiral Husband E. Kimmel, had told his staff: "Declaration of war might be preceded by a surprise attack on Pearl Harbor."

"Magic," of course, continued to sound the signal of increasing danger. September 24, Tokyo to its Honolulu consulate general: "With regard to warships and aircraft carriers, report on those at anchor, tied up at wharves, buoys and in docks." November 29: "Report even when there are no [ship] movements."

That same day, Chief of Naval Operations Admiral Harold "Betty" Stark notified his Hawaii, Philippine and Panama commanders from Washington: "This is a war warning. An aggressive move by Japan is expected within the next few days." Indeed from Tokyo, December 3, came a further indication—"In view of present situation, let me know day by day if there are any observation balloons above Pearl Harbor"—and on December 5 the FBI in Hawaii warned Pearl that the Japanese consulate was burning its confidential papers. The next evening, December 6, F.D.R. soberly read the intercept of the first 13 parts of a climactic Tokyo message to envoys Nomura and Kurusu, breaking off negotiations forthwith. Said F.D.R. to Harry Hopkins: "This means war."

In the heaving, trackless North Pacific the silent striking force received the go signal: "Climb Mt. Niitaka." By 8 a.m. December 7 (2:30 a.m. in Hawaii) the men assigned to monitoring "Magic" in Washington decoded the 14th

The oily, black smoke of war rises from the wreckage of the Naval Air Station at Pearl Harbor. The Japanese attackers lost fewer than 100 men.

and final part of Japan's message to its emissaries: "It is impossible to reach an agreement. Submit to the U.S. government our reply at 1 p.m. on the seventh, your time."

War within the next few hours—but where? An Army colonel and a Navy commander involved in "Magic" both remarked that 1 p.m. in Washington was just after dawn at Pearl, the quiet time when crews were piped to breakfast. Panama and other possible danger spots had gone on full alert after the November 27 warning: airfields blacked out, radars in continuous operation, fighter planes and antiaircraft guns in readiness.

But at the prime objective—the home base of the fleet that was the greatest single deterrent to Japanese aggression and therefore the most logical point of attack—the Army, which was responsible for defending the base, put itself on the mildest of its three alerts, the No. 1 or antisabotage alert. This order parked the planes in bunches, the easier to guard them against sabotage (and the easier to bomb them). Antiaircraft guns were retained in parks, and ammunition in magazines, so that getting the guns into action would take one to four hours. Hawaii's five mobile radars operated not 24 hours daily but from 4 a.m. to 11 a.m. weekdays and from 4 a.m. to 7 a.m. weekends —weekends being days of rest at Pearl as in civilian U.S.

The Navy at Pearl also put itself on its loosest alert —Condition Three, meaning that but 25 per cent of its antiaircraft guns were manned. There were no barrage balloons, no torpedo nets, no reconnaissance planes. Virtually all fleet units were brought into Pearl and conveniently moored side by side. One third to one half the ships' officers were ashore.

Still, there was a little time to get set—and a host of 11th-hour warnings. At 6:45 a.m. December 7, the destroyer *Ward* radioed that it had ferreted out a Japanese midget sub and sunk it, firing what turned out to be the first American shot in the Pacific war. At 7:02 two soldiers, voluntarily staying overtime to train on one of the Army's five radar screens, reported seeing blips. None of these warnings was taken up. "Hell," said one officer of the radar blips, "it's probably just a pigeon with a metal band

around its leg." The attackers were 50 minutes away.

"Pearl Harbor was still asleep in the morning mist," the commander of the lead Japanese formation recalled later. At 7:55 as the first of three attacking waves began its run, of 96 vessels at Pearl, one lone destroyer was under way. With the first bombs, hoarse klaxons calling General Quarters on every vessel shattered the Sabbath quiet and sounded the end of peace for the next 1,364 days. In 110 minutes eight big battleships and three light cruisers were sunk or damaged, 188 planes destroyed and 2,400 men killed. The Japanese accomplished this at a cost of 29 aircraft, five midget submarines and one fleet sub. They had expected to lose one third of the attack fleet. They lost none; their fleet was not even detected.

The blow not only paralyzed U.S. power in the Pacific for the greater part of a crucial year, it also laid bare America's inexcusable optimism and its unbelievable unreadiness for battle. The U.S. had had every possible warning. Yet when attack came, hardly an American failed to express stunned surprise. In Washington, as he received the first word of the raid, Navy Secretary Knox, who had warned of just such an attack the year before, blurted: "My God! This can't be true. This must mean the Philippines." "No sir," said Admiral Stark. "This is Pearl."

Before decade's end, six investigations would try to clarify what had happened and why. But despite 40 volumes of testimony, the whole affair would remain essentially a mystery. And the question would stick forever in the American craw: How could Pearl Harbor have happened?

Before America got ready for what lay ahead those next four years, there would be other bloody illustrations of the military's aptitude for what soon became known as the snafu (translated, bowdlerized, as Situation Normal, All Fouled Up). Just 10 hours after Pearl, with the Americans now fully alerted, there was a second surprise attack of almost equal magnitude. Japanese planes sweeping in from the north caught General Douglas MacArthur with his planes down and in some 80 minutes destroyed half the U.S. air arm in the Philippines. The Japanese lost seven fighters. The United States lost its innocence.

Where Were You When the Bombs Fell?

At 2:20 p.m. Washington time, 55 minutes after the attack started, White House Press Secretary Steve Early, at home in pajamas, got the press services simultaneously on the phone and released the news. That instant, like the snap of a camera's shutter, froze the American scene:

A commander on the bridge of the U.S.S. *Ramapo* banged away at the planes with a pistol. Tears laced his cheeks. A bosun's mate threw wrenches at the low-flying aircraft. From the magazine came a call asking what he needed. *"Powder,"* he yelled. *"I can't keep throwing things at them."*

Seaman Joseph Hydruska, 22, boarded the U.S.S. *Oklahoma*, which had taken six torpedoes below the waterline and was about to capsize. *"I was terribly afraid. We were cutting through with acetylene torches. First we found six naked men waist deep in water. They didn't know how long they had been down there and they were crying and moaning with pain. Some of them were very badly wounded. We could hear tapping all over the ship, SOS taps, no voices, just those eerie taps from all over. There was nothing we could do for most of them."*

A sergeant in the 27th Infantry at Pearl refused to issue ammunition. He pointed to a sign that said no ammunition without captain's orders.

The explosions awoke *Christian Science Monitor* correspondent Joseph Harsch in a Honolulu hotel. He thought how much it sounded like the air raids in Berlin, where he had been last year, and woke his wife: *"Darling, you've often asked what an air raid sounds like. Listen to this—it's a good imitation." "Oh, so that's what it's like,"* she said. They both dozed off again.

On the U.S.S. *San Francisco* a young engineer came topside and said to an ensign: *"Thought I'd come up and die with you."*

The gunners on the U.S.S. *Argonne* shot down their own antenna.

Battery B on Oahu was issued machine-gun ammunition dated 1918—so old the belts fell apart in the loading machines.

Near the married men's quarters at Pearl a gang of children jumped up and down screaming, *"Here come the Indians."*

Seaman "Squash" Marshall raced for cover from strafers at Kaneohe air station. As bullets snapped at his heels he actually seemed to outrun a Zero for 100 yards, then zagged to one side while the bullets pinged ahead. The men watching set up a great cheer as though he had made a touchdown.

Water swirled into the U.S.S. *California*, where Machinist's Mate Robert Scott in the forward air compressor station was trying to feed air to the 5-inch guns. The others ran, yelling to Scott to get out in a hurry. He shouted: *"This is my station—I'll stay here and give them air as long as the guns are going."* They let him have his way and shut the watertight door.

Dashing to get a better look at the bombing, a Honolulu man yelled at a reporter: *"The mainland papers will exaggerate this."*

An hour after an appeal for blood, 500 volunteers swamped Dr. John Devereux and three assistants at the Honolulu blood bank; they ran out of containers and used sterilized Coke bottles. Devereux's best volunteer, cleaning bottles and tubes, was a local prostitute.

Admiral Kimmel's orderly came out of the admiral's office at Pearl and said: *"He's tearing his hair out, saying 'What should I do, what should I do?' "*

In Pearl a wounded ensign begged a friend, *"Kill me."*

On the U.S.S. *New Orleans* at Pearl, Chaplain Howell Forgy told the gun crews he was sorry they didn't have church that morning but to *"praise the Lord and pass the ammunition."*

General Jonathan Wainwright in the Philippines jiggled the phone to get his aide. *"Johnny!" "Hello. . . . Yes, General." "The cat has jumped."*

Winston Churchill placed a phone call. *"Mr. President, what's this about Japan?" "It's quite true,"* said F.D.R. *"We're all in the same boat." "This actually simplifies things,"* said Churchill. *"God be with you."* He went to bed and slept soundly.

People in Phoenix phoned *The Arizona Republic* newsroom and asked: *"Have you got any score on the game between the Chicago Bears and the Cardinals? Aren't you getting anything besides that war stuff?"*

Ernest Vogt and his family continued eating their Sunday roast chicken dinner in New York City. *"I thought it was another Orson Welles hoax."*

A pretty, black-haired girl complained in Palm Springs: *"Everybody knew this was going to happen, so why spoil a perfectly good Sunday afternoon worrying about it?"*

In Pittsburgh, where Senator Gerald Nye had gone to address 2,500 hysterically isolationist America Firsters, a newsman told him of the attack on Pearl. Nye snapped: *"Sounds terribly fishy to me."*

At nightfall a sentry at Schofield Barracks near Pearl challenged three times, got no answer and shot one of his own mules.

Edward R. Murrow had been invited to dinner with the President that evening. His wife phoned the White House: were they still expected? Eleanor Roosevelt said: *"We all have to eat. Come anyway."* Later that night the President pounded the study table as he described to Murrow how the U.S. planes were destroyed *"on the ground, by God, on the ground."*

Ensign John F. Kennedy, U.S.N.R., was at Griffith Stadium in Washington watching the Redskins win, 20-14, over the Philadelphia Eagles. The Stadium did not give the news over the loudspeaker. Young Kennedy heard it over the car radio going home and immediately put in for active sea duty.

At a newsstand at Michigan and Randolph in Chicago, a fat woman saw the headlines and said: *"What's this?" "We're at war lady, for crying out loud." "Well, what do you know,"* she said. *"Who with?"*

F.D.R. called secretary Grace Tully into his study and started dictating: *"Yesterday comma December seven comma nineteen forty-one dash a date which will live in infamy dash."*

At Fort Sam Houston, a brigadier general catching up on sleep after weeks of tough field maneuvers got a phone call and his wife heard him say: *"Yes? When? I'll be right down."* As he rushed off, Dwight Eisenhower told Mamie he was going to headquarters and didn't know when he would be back.

Combat - The Island War

No sooner had the U.S. managed to accept the shocking reality of Pearl Harbor than Americans were faced with another grim circumstance they had never experienced in all the nation's history: continuing defeat on the battlefield. From December 7, 1941, on deep into 1942, America and the Allies endured a series of disasters—Guam, Wake, Hong Kong, Borneo, Singapore, the Netherlands Indies, and most agonizing of all for America, the surrender of the Philippines *(right)*. Not until late 1942 were the Allies able to start onto the offensive. When the flow of war finally did shift, the initial U.S. victories were won in the island war —where the first bitter defeats had been suffered. In the months that followed, Marines and GIs tightened an iron noose around Japan by leapfrogging from one obscure Pacific outcropping to another: Guadalcanal, Tarawa, Eniwetok, Saipan, Ulithi, Iwo Jima, Okinawa. All told, American troops launched more than 100 island invasions, 68 of them involving heavy losses. At Iwo Jima alone, every unit committed suffered at least 50 per cent casualties. "I hope to God," muttered one wounded Marine in a fitting epitaph to the costly conquest of Iwo Jima, "that we don't have to go on any more of those screwy islands."

☆ ☆ ☆ ☆ ☆ ☆ ☆ ☆ ☆ ☆ ☆ ☆ ☆ ☆ ☆ ☆ ☆ ☆

GIs on Bataan surrender to the Japanese, who search them for weapons.

In a field hospital, doctors dig shrapnel from a GI's back.

Always the rain and the mud, torrid heat and teeming
insect life, the stink of rotten jungle and rotting dead; malaria
burning the body and fungus infection eating away the
feet, and no hot chow for weeks. And fury by day and terror
by night and utter weariness all the time. And death.

MAJOR FRANK O. HOUGH, U.S. MARINE CORPS

A dead soldier lies where the tide has left him on Buna beach.

75

A GI under enemy shellfire huddles in a ditch on Okinawa.

That artillery did things to you. We'd been
told not to duck when we heard the screaming of shells;
it would be too late. But we ducked anyway.
Even the almost silent pop of the mortars was frightening.
We got to know exactly where a shell would land.

A CORPORAL QUOTED IN THE GI NEWSPAPER *YANK*

Protected by naval gunfire, GIs invade Makin Island.

We You Coming-To-Get, Yank

*The terrors of island warfare were apotheosized in
the novel "The Naked and the Dead" by ex-GI Norman Mailer.
In the excerpt below, Mailer's island is fictitious,
but the experience of his Sergeant Croft was brutally real.*

Croft stared tensely across the river. The moon had come out, and the strands of beach on either side of the stream were shining with a silver glow. The jungle wall on the other side looked impenetrable.

The mortars fired again behind him with a cruel flat sound. He watched the shells land in the jungle, and then creep nearer to the river in successive volleys. A mortar answered from the Japanese side of the river, and about a quarter of a mile to the left Croft could hear several machine guns spattering at each other, the uproar deep and regular. . . .

His ears were keyed to all the sounds of the night, and from long experience he sifted out the ones that were meaningless. If an animal rustled in its hole, he paid no attention; if some crickets chirped, his ear disregarded them. Now he picked a muffled slithering sound which he knew could be made only by men moving through a thin patch of jungle. . . .

Croft's mouth tightened. His hand felt for the bolt of the machine gun, and he slowly brought it to bear on the coconut grove. The rustling grew louder; it seemed as if men were creeping through the brush on the other side of the river to a point opposite his gun. Croft swallowed once. Tiny charges seemed to pulse through his limbs and his head was as empty and shockingly aware as if it had been plunged into a pail of freezing water. . . .

Then he heard a sound which pierced his flesh. Someone called from across the river, "Yank! Yank!" Croft sat numb. The voice was thin and high-pitched, hideous in a whisper. "That's a Jap," Croft told himself. He was incapable of moving for that instant.

"Yank!" It was calling to him. "Yank. We you coming-to-get, Yank."

The night lay like a heavy stifling mat over the river. Croft tried to breathe. "We you coming-to-get, Yank."

Croft felt as if a hand had suddenly clapped against his back, traveled up his spine over his skull to clutch at the hair on his forehead. "Coming to get you, Yank," he heard himself whisper. He had the agonizing frustration of a man in a nightmare who wants to scream and cannot utter a sound. "We you coming-to-get, Yank."

He shivered terribly for a moment, and his hands seemed congealed on the machine gun. He could not bear the intense pressure in his head.

"We you coming-to-get, Yank," the voice screamed.

"COME AND GET ME YOU SONSOFBITCHES," Croft roared. . . .

"Oh, we come, Yank, we come."

Croft pulled back the bolt on his machine gun, and rammed it home. His heart was still beating with frenzy "Recon . . . RECON, UP ON THE LINE," he shouted with all his strength.

A machine gun lashed at him from across the river, and he ducked in his hole. In the darkness it spat a vindictive white light like an acetylene torch, and its sound was terrifying. Croft was holding himself together by the force of his will. He pressed the trigger of his gun and it leaped and bucked under his hand.

The tracers spewed wildly into the jungle on the other side of the river.

But the noise, the vibration of his gun, calmed him. He directed it to where he had seen the Japanese gunfire and loosed a volley. The handle pounded against his fist, and he had to steady it with both hands. The hot metallic smell of the barrel eddied back to him, made what he was doing real again. He ducked in his hole waiting for the reply and winced involuntarily as the bullets whipped past. . . .

Croft fired the gun again, held it for a long vicious burst, and then ducked in his hole. An awful scream singed the night, and for an instant Croft grinned weakly. Got him, he thought. . . .

"RECON, UP. . . UP!" he shouted furiously and fired steadily for ten seconds to cover their advance. As he paused he could hear some men crawling behind him, and he whispered, "Recon?"

"Yeah." Gallagher dropped into the hole with him. "Mother of Mary," he muttered. Croft could feel him shaking beside him.

"Stop it!" he gripped his arm tensely. "The other men up?"

"Yeah." . . .

Croft picked up his flare gun. The firing had not abated, but through it he heard someone shouting in Japanese. He pointed the gun in the air.

"Here they come," Croft said.

He fired the flare and shouted, "STOP 'EM!"

A shrill cry came out of the jungle across the river. It was the scream a man might utter if his foot was being crushed. "AAIIIIII, AAAIIIIIIIII."

The flare burst at the moment the Japanese started their charge. Croft had a split perception of the Japanese machine gun firing from a flank, and then he began to fire automatically, not looking where he fired, but holding his gun low, swinging it from side to side. . . .

The line of men who charged across the river began to fall. In the water they were slowed considerably and the concentrated fire from recon's side raged at them like a wind across an open field. They began to stumble over the bodies ahead of them. Croft saw one soldier reach into the air behind another's body as though trying to clutch something in the sky and Croft fired at him for what seemed many seconds before the arm collapsed. . . .

Croft fired and fired, switching targets with the quick reflexes of an athlete shifting for a ball. As soon as he saw men falling he would attack another group. The line of Japanese broke into little bunches of men who wavered, began to retreat.

The light of the flare went out and Croft was blinded for a moment. There was no sound again in the darkness and he fumbled for another flare, feeling an almost desperate urgency. . . . Croft's hand found the flare box, and he loaded the gun again. He was beginning to see in the darkness, and he hesitated. But something moved on the river and he fired the flare. As it burst, a few Japanese soldiers were caught motionless in the water. Croft pivoted his gun on them and fired. One of the soldiers remained standing for an incredible time. There was no expression on his face; he looked vacant and surprised even as the bullets struck him in the chest.

Nothing was moving now on the river. In the light of the flare, the bodies looked as limp and unhuman as bags of grain. One soldier began to float downstream, his face in the water. On the beach near the gun, another Japanese soldier was lying on his back. A wide stain of blood was spreading out from his body, and his stomach, ripped open, gaped like the swollen entrails of a fowl. On an impulse Croft fired a burst into him, and felt a twitch of pleasure as he saw the body quiver.

The Sea War

Although the Japanese bombing of Pearl Harbor destroyed or crippled 18 naval ships, including eight battleships, the disaster of December 7 pointed the way toward eventual U.S. victory. For even the most myopic old-line admiral could recognize in Pearl Harbor the power of carrier-based aircraft. From that time forward, carriers replaced battleships as the U.S. Navy's chief offensive weapon, thus revolutionizing warfare at sea.

The pattern for this new brand of sea war was set just six months after Pearl, in a weird, sprawling struggle in which, one Navy man wrote, "Nine tenths of the men engaged never saw the prize for which they fought." That prize was American-held Midway Island, which a Japanese armada was attempting to seize. The battle for Midway began on June 3, 1942, when the two fleets were 400 miles apart. For three days, great flights of bombers attacked each other's seagoing bases. On June 6, when the fleets finally disengaged, 403 planes had been shot down, 253 of them Japanese. Even more significant, the U.S. fleet had sunk four enemy carriers and lost only one, and Midway was safe. The reduction of Japan's navy was far from complete, but Admiral Chester Nimitz had grounds for making a jubilant pun: "We are about midway to that objective."

A sailor paints a fresh kill on a carrier scoreboard.

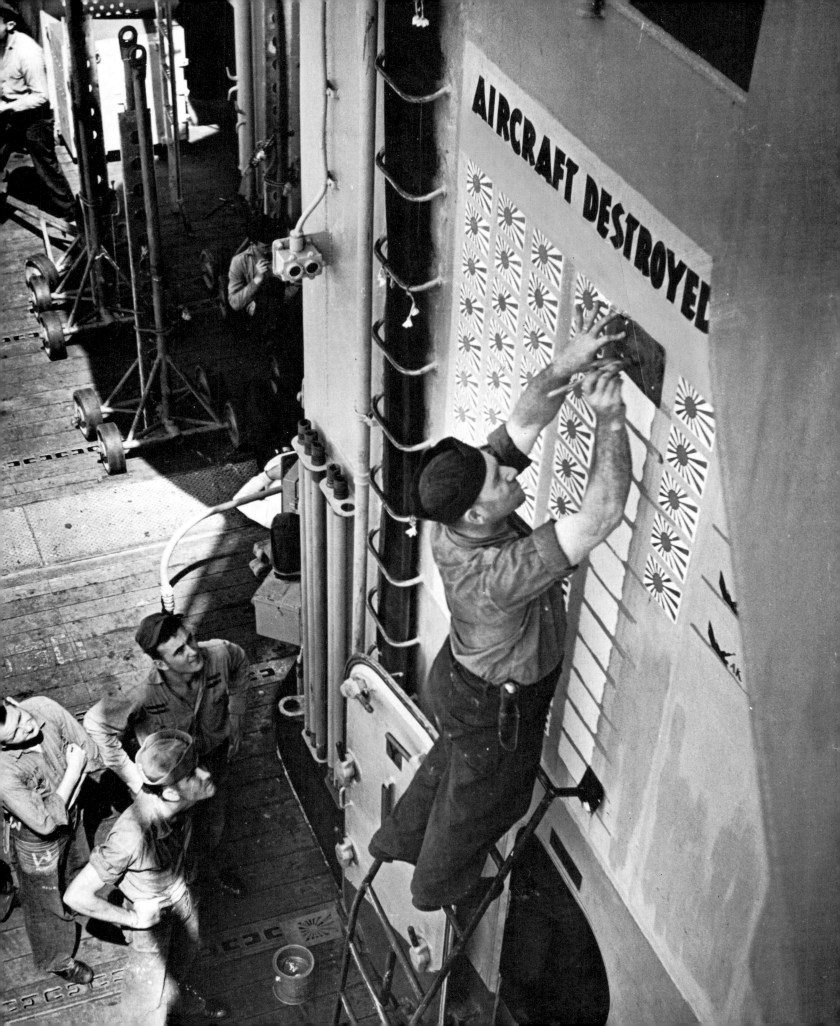

Crewmen ease over the side of the sinking carrier "Lexington" in the Battle of the Coral Sea.

At *sunset, in a very orderly fashion the men—reluctantly—were*
taken off to destroyers and cruisers. They were so calm that some of them went below and filled
their helmets with ice cream from the ship's stores, and went overside eating. All
arranged their shoes in an orderly row on the flight deck before leaving. No lives were lost at
all in the water. All our casualties came from the combat or fire fighting.

REAR ADMIRAL FREDERICK C. SHERMAN, CAPTAIN OF THE *LEXINGTON*

A Japanese bomber, hit by gunfire from the carrier "Hornet," bursts into flame.

Planes seem to be completely around us. . . . Fire on water
off our port beam. That's one Jap down off our port quarter now. . . . They
are using flares. . . . We are holding field day: Another Jap
down. . . . Another. . . . One ship hit with torpedo. . . . Has regained steering
control, everything O.K. . . . 0125: The moon set—Thank God.
RADIO MESSAGES FROM U.S. SHIPS OFF KWAJALEIN

Crewmen on the "Hornet" watch the onrush of Japanese planes.

The "Borie's" Last Battle

"Time" correspondent John Hersey reported a battle between the destroyer "Borie," commanded by Lt. Charles H. Hutchins, and a German U-boat in the Atlantic. This excerpt begins just after the sub was forced to surface.

Hutchins raised his right arm and roared to his helmsman. The searchlight flared on. This lit up the sleek gray target, but it also gave the Germans something to shoot at. Germans came scrambling out of the conning tower, manning the machine guns. As each German ran to a gun, he would be horribly killed.

The "Borie" caught up with the German and began to pull ahead. Hutchins shouted: "All stations stand by for ram!"

Men on the destroyer braced themselves for the pleasure and the shock. There was no shock, no crunching noise. Instead a huge wave lifted the "Borie's" bow high and put it down gently on the deck of the submarine, just forward of the conning tower. Thus the two ships, scarcely damaged, came to rest, bow over bow, locked in a mortal "V."

Disappointment at once gave way to crazy elation. Hutchins roared: "Fire! Fire! Open fire!" Men threw their arms around each other and danced. Executive Officer Brown stood there, waiting coolly until a German torso lifted itself, then raising his tommy gun like a professor raising a pointer at a black-board, and pulling the trigger. . . . Finally, 10 minutes after the ramming, the two ships worked free of each other. Then the incredible contest began again. The U-boat went into a tight left circle and the "Borie" did too. Hutchins turned out his light, hoping the U-boat would try sneaking out of the circle. The submarine did just that. Hutchins snapped on the light again and found the glistening U-boat streaking off. The "Borie" pursued.

All through the battle so far the "Borie" had been to the right of its adversary. Hutchins decided to break through to the other side, so while he chased the enemy he pulled left. And now he gave an order which helped to win the battle. He ordered depth charges set shallow. The submarine again held its course until the last moment. But this time, instead of turning sharply away, the German turned sharply toward the "Borie." The U-boat captain had decided to ram the destroyer.

Hutchins had one of his flashes of combat genius. He ordered hard left, ordered the starboard engine stopped, the port engine backed full. This threw the ship into a skidding stop, with the stern swinging toward the oncoming sub. At the right moment, Hutchins shouted: "Okay, give 'em the starboard battery."

Three round shapes arched and fell within feet of the submarine —two on one side and one on the other. They went off shallow. The submarine lurched out of the water like a hurt mammal and came to a stop very close to the "Borie's" flank.

Somehow the submarine managed to start up. It was like a dying animal—a good Spanish bull that refuses to die. It slipped astern of the "Borie" and shot off at an angle. By this time the Americans were dazed by the stubbornness of the enemy.

The 4-inch gunners gave the U-boat its final blow. They hit the starboard Diesel exhaust again. The Germans huddled on the conning tower. Gun Captain Reynolds got off one last round. It blew the bridge structure, with all its occupants, right off the U-boat. Water poured into the submarine, its bow lifted as the ship slipped under the waves and exploded horribly. After one hour and four minutes of tenacious fighting, the submarine sank.

The Air War

Until the final year of the war, the only direct attack the English and Americans could mount upon Germany was through the air; and to do even that proved difficult, costly and harrowing. Hundreds of American planes were lost in the Atlantic crossing as freighters were sunk by German U-boats. Of the planes that reached Europe, 18,500 bombers and fighters—and 64,000 airmen—were shot down by Luftwaffe fighters and German antiaircraft batteries. The lives of the pilots and crewmen were one long series of contrasts: periods of easy routine on countryside bases, then the hours of tension on the missions. Many men cracked under the strain.

The air war reached its fierce crescendo early in 1944. Fed by the booming output of U.S. factories, the big fleets of Flying Fortress and Liberator bombers swelled into 1,000-plane armadas, and their losses were sharply reduced by convoys of long-range American fighter planes. Within a few months, these vast fighter-bomber flights had not only pounded German war plants and dozens of cities, but had virtually obliterated the Luftwaffe. Fortress Europe now lay vulnerable to attack by sea, and General Eisenhower could promise his invasion forces, "If you see fighting aircraft over you, they will be ours."

A weary crewman grabs a bite at an English base.

An all-Negro fighter group gets its orders at a base in Italy.

In the briefing room, I felt a sting of anticipation as I
stared at the red string on the map that stretched from our base
in England to a pin point deep in Germany. . . .

. . . Our bombs were away. I looked back and saw a beautiful
sight—a rectangular pillar of smoke rising.
Even from this great height I could see that we had smeared
the objective. The price? Cheap. 200 airmen.

LIEUTENANT COLONEL BEIRNE LAY JR.

A Flying Fortress passes over a burning target in Peenemünde, Germany.

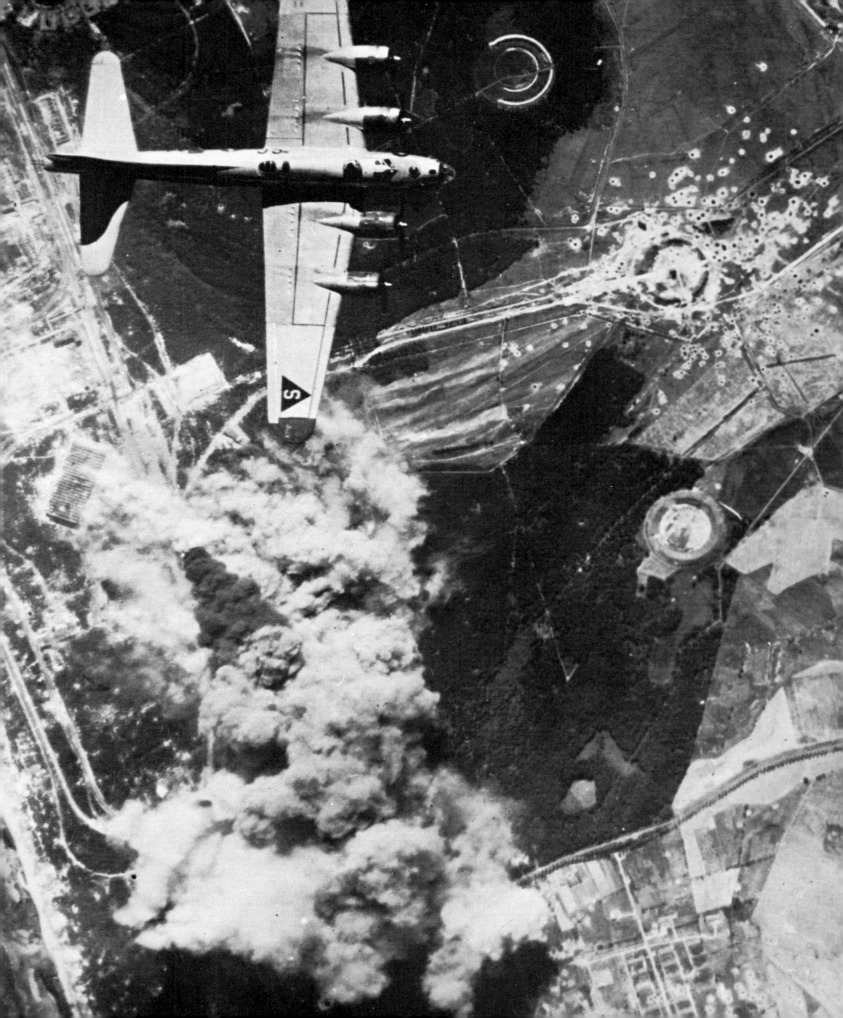

Vigil at a Bomber Base

*The tension of the air war over Europe was felt
not only by the fliers, but also by the ground crews who waited
for their birds to return. One such vigil is described
below in an adaptation of a report by novelist John Steinbeck.*

The field is deserted after the ships have left. The ground crew go into barracks to get some sleep, because they have been working most of the night. In the hangars repair crews are working over ships that have been injured. The crews own a number of small dogs. Now these dogs wander disconsolately about the field. The life has gone out of the bomber station. The morning passes slowly. The squadron was due over the target at 9:52. As 9:50 comes and passes you have the ships in your mind. Now the flak has come up at them. Perhaps now a swarm of fighters has hurled itself at them. The thing happens in your mind.

The crew last night had told a story of the death of a Fortress. The formation was flying toward St. Nazaire and the air was very clear. Then the flak came up, they said, and some Messerschmitts parked off out of range and began to pot at them with their cannon. They didn't see where the Fortress was hit. But the Fortress slowly nosed up and up until she tried to climb vertically and, of course, she couldn't. Then she slipped in slow motion, backing like a falling leaf, balanced for a while and then her nose edged over and she started for the ground.

The crew could see the gunner trying to get out and then he did, and his parachute fluffed open. And the ball-turret gunner —they could see him flopping about. "Mary Ruth's" crew was yelling, "Get out, you pilots." The ship must have been almost to the ground when two little puffs of white shot out of her. And the crew yelled with relief. And then the ship hit the ground.

Beside the No. 1 hangar there is a little mound of earth covered with short, heavy grass. At 12:15 the ground men begin to congregate on it and sweat out the homecoming. Rumor comes with the crew chief that they have reported, but it is rumor. A small dog, which might be a gray Scottie if his ears didn't hang down and his tail bend the wrong way, comes to sit on the little mound. He stretches out and puts his whiskery muzzle on his outstretched paws. All the ground crews are there now, waiting for their ships. It is the longest set of minutes imaginable.

Suddenly the little dog raises his head. His body begins to tremble all over. The crew chief has a pair of field glasses. "Can't see anything yet," he says. The little dog continues to shudder.

And here they come. You can just see the dots far to the south. The formation is good, but one ship flies alone and ahead. "Can you see her number? Who is she?" The lead ship drops altitude and comes in straight for the field. From her side two little rockets break, a red one and a white one. The ambulance starts down the runway. There is a hurt man on that ship.

The main formation comes over the field and each ship peels to circle for a landing, but the lone ship drops and the wheels strike the ground and the Fortress lands like a great bug on the runway. But the moment her wheels are on the ground there is a sharp, crying bark and a streak of gray. The little dog seems hardly to touch the ground. He streaks across the field toward the landed ship. One by one the Fortresses land and the ground crews check off the numbers. "Mary Ruth" is there. Only one ship is missing and she landed farther south, with short fuel tanks. There is a great sigh of relief on the mound. The mission is over.

The Land War

The basic premise of Allied grand strategy was that Germany could not finally be defeated until her land armies were destroyed. To put troops on the continent, the Western allies first invaded North Africa, in November 1942; within a year they had leapfrogged to Sicily and thence to southern Italy. Meanwhile even greater forces were being marshaled at English bases for a cross-Channel invasion. By May 1944, Britain was jammed with 2,876,000 troops—most of them American—and with millions of tons of supplies and equipment.

The materiel for the invasion was enormously sophisticated —multiple rocket-launchers, amphibious tanks, huge floating docks. Yet the basic unit for this modern assault was an old stand-by: the ordinary foot soldier, simply equipped with a rifle and ammunition, carrying the few other things he needed to survive, relying heavily on personal courage and resourcefulness. The rifleman alone could take enemy positions inaccessible to tanks and irreducible by air attack; and the primary purpose of the whole prodigious invasion build-up was to put 176,000 such troops onto German-held beaches on the first day of direct combat. When D-Day finally dawned on the historic morning of June 6, 1944, it was really I-Day—infantryman's day.

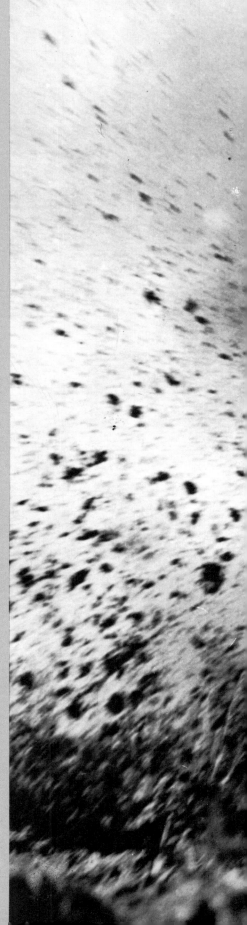

Beneath a shellburst, a paratrooper attacks in Holland.

Ike offers a last word to paratroopers before the D-Day takeoff.

A Touch of Ike

On June 5, 1944, General Dwight D. Eisenhower sent a message (below) to the vast Allied expeditionary force, urging all to victory in the invasion of France on the next day. Ike also scribbled a draft (bottom), never sent, assuming personal responsibility in case of failure.

You are about to embark upon the Great Crusade, toward which we have striven these many months. The eyes of the world are upon you. The hopes and prayers of liberty-loving people everywhere march with you. In company with our brave Allies and brothers-in-arms on other Fronts, you will bring about the destruction of the German war machine, the elimination of Nazi tyranny over the oppressed peoples of Europe, and security for ourselves in a free world.

Your task will not be an easy one. Your enemy is well trained, well equipped and battle-hardened. He will fight savagely.

But this is the year 1944! . . . The tide has turned! The free men of the world are marching together to Victory!

I have full confidence in your courage, devotion to duty and skill in battle. We will accept nothing less than full Victory!

Good Luck! And let us all beseech the blessing of Almighty God upon this great and noble undertaking.

Our landings in the Cherbourg-Havre area have failed to gain a satisfactory foothold and I have withdrawn the troops. My decision to attack at this time and place was based upon the best information available. The troops, the air and the Navy did all that bravery and devotion to duty could do. If any blame or fault attaches to the attempt it is mine alone.

On D-Day, GIs leave an LCT and wade ashore into enemy fire on Omaha Beach, Normandy.

The boat pulls in until it can't move any more, and then you step out
and it is only one foot deep. Then you move farther in and—plop—you're over your head.

"If you want to live, keep moving," everybody said. Nobody walked. They came
in running fast, falling flat, hunting for a big rock, a shellhole, anything. Then digging in.

VETERANS OF D-DAY

A Lovely Day for a Stroll

The favorite war correspondent of the GIs was skinny, gray-haired Ernie Pyle, who had shared with them the front-line hazards of North Africa, Sicily and Italy. Pyle's report on the aftermath of D-Day is excerpted below.

I took a walk along the historic coast of Normandy in the country of France. It was a lovely day for strolling along the seashore. Men were sleeping on the sand, some of them sleeping forever. Men were floating in the water, but they didn't know they were in the water, for they were dead. . . .

I walked for a mile and a half along the water's edge of our many-miled invasion beach. I walked slowly, for the detail on that beach was infinite.

The wreckage was vast and startling. The awful waste and destruction of war, even aside from the loss of human life, has always been one of its outstanding features to those who are in it. Anything and everything is expendable. And we did expend on our beachhead in Normandy during those first few hours.

There were trucks tipped half over and swamped, partly sunken barges, and the angled-up corners of jeeps, and small landing craft half submerged . . . you could still see those vicious six-pronged iron snares that helped snag and wreck them. . . .

But there was another and more human litter. It extended in a thin little line, just like a high-water mark, for miles along the beach. This was the strewn personal gear, gear that would never be needed again by those who fought and died to give us our entrance into Europe.

There in a jumbled row for mile on mile were soldiers' packs. There were socks and shoe polish, sewing kits, diaries, Bibles, hand grenades. There were the latest letters from home . . .

I picked up a pocket Bible with a soldier's name in it, and put it in my jacket. I carried it half a mile or so and then put it back down on the beach. I don't know why I picked it up, or why I put it down again.

Soldiers carry strange things ashore with them. In every invasion there is at least one soldier hitting the beach at H-hour with a banjo slung over his shoulder. The most ironic piece of equipment marking our beach—this beach first of despair, then of victory—was a tennis racket that some soldier had brought along. It lay lonesomely on the sand, clamped in its press, not a string broken.

Over and around this long thin line of personal anguish, fresh men were rushing vast supplies to keep our armies pushing into France. Other squads of men picked amidst the wreckage to salvage ammunition and equipment that was still usable.

Men worked and slept on the beach for days before the last D-Day victim was taken away for burial.

I stepped over the form of one youngster whom I thought dead. But when I looked down I saw he was only sleeping. He was very young, and very tired. He lay on one elbow, his hand suspended in the air about six inches from the ground. And in the palm of his hand he held a large, smooth rock.

I stood and looked at him for a long time. He seemed in his sleep to hold that rock lovingly, as though it were his last link with a vanishing world. I have no idea at all why he went to sleep with the rock in his hand, or what kept him from dropping it once he was asleep. It was just one of those little things without explanation that a person remembers for a long time.

A paratrooper rescues a wounded buddy.

We have stopped cold everything that has been
thrown at us from the north, east,
southwest . . . four German Panzer Divisions, two German
Infantry Divisions and one German
Paratroop Division. We continue to hold Bastogne. . . .
We are giving our country and
our loved ones at home a worthy Christmas present.

GENERAL ANTHONY MC AULIFFE, CHRISTMAS 1944

GIs trapped in Bastogne show weariness during their eight-day siege.

103

The War

In March 1945 victorious riflemen in Germany press on toward the Rhine.

It's almost over and I'm almost home and I'm scared that maybe just a
lucky shot will get me. And I don't want to die now, not
when it's almost over. I don't want to die now. Do you know what I mean?

A SOLDIER QUOTED IN *YANK—THE GI STORY OF THE WAR*

Army Air Forces

ARMY AIR FORCES
Headquarters insignia is basic design for other AAF patches

MEDITERRANEAN ALLIED AIR FORCE
Composed of U.S. and British air commands, fought over southern Europe

U.S. STRATEGIC AIR FORCE
Made up of U.S. 8th, 15th Air Forces, directed heavy bomber raids over Europe

FIRST AIR FORCE
Headquarters at Mitchel Field N.Y., protects Atlantic Seaboard

SECOND AIR FORCE
Headquarters at Colorado Springs, protects western U.S.

THIRD AIR FORCE
Headquarters at Tampa, Florida, protects southeastern U.S.

FOURTH AIR FORCE
Headquarters at San Francisco, protects U.S. Far West

FIFTH AIR FORCE
Headquarters in the Philippines, patrols Southwest Pacific

SIXTH AIR FORCE
Headquarters in Canal Zone, protects Caribbean area

SEVENTH AIR FORCE
Headquarters in Marianas, covers Central Pacific

EIGHTH AIR FORCE
Headquarters in England, carried out heavy bomber raids over Europe

NINTH AIR FORCE
Headquarters in England, carried out tactical raids over Europe

TENTH AIR FORCE
Headquarters in India, covers India-Burma area

ELEVENTH AIR FORCE
Headquarters in Aleutians, covers Northern Pacific

TWELFTH AIR FORCE
Headquarters in Italy, carried out tactical Mediterranean raids

THIRTEENTH AIR FORCE
Headquarters in Southwest Pacific, covers this area

FOURTEENTH AIR FORCE
Headquarters in Chungking, covers China

FIFTEENTH AIR FORCE
Headquarters in Italy, carried out strategic Mediterranean raids

TWENTIETH AIR FORCE
Headquarters in Washington, D.C., is superbomber force against Japan

Armored Divisions

1st
Oran, Bizerte, Cassino, Anzio, Rome, Milan

2nd "HELL ON WHEELS"
Morocco, Sicily, Normandy, Houffalize, Westphalia

3rd "SPEARHEAD"
St. Lô, Battle of the Bulge, Cologne, Ruhr pocket

4th
Normandy breakthrough, Nancy, Coblenz, the Saar

5th "VICTORY"
Normandy, Hürtgen Forest, Trier

6th "SUPER SIXTH"
Brest, Normandy breakthrough, Bastogne, the Saar

7th "LUCKY SEVENTH"
Metz, St. Vith, the Ruhr

8th "THUNDERING HERD"
Cologne, Duisberg, northeast across Germany

9th
Battle of the Bulge, St. Vith, Remagen bridgehead

10th "TIGER"
Bastogne, Trier, Ulm, Bavaria, Austrian Tyrol

11th
Bastogne, Siegfried Line, Leipzig, Austria

12th
Colmar, Nuremberg, Danube, Munich

13th
Ruhr pocket, Regensburg, Danube and Isar Rivers

14th
Southern France, Siegfried Line, Austria, Czechoslovakia

ARMY GROUND FORCES
Trains, organizes and equips
Ground Force units

ARMORED CENTER AND UNITS
Insignia for Armored Force
Headquarters and Headquarters Company

**AGF REPLACEMENT
DEPOTS**
Handles troop
replacements

**REPLACEMENT AND
SCHOOL COMMAND**
Trains infantry, cavalry
and artillery personnel

**ANTIAIRCRAFT
COMMAND**
Trains AA personnel

**AIRBORNE
COMMAND**
Trains airborne units

ARMY SERVICE FORCES
Provides services and supplies
for all Army units

PORTS OF EMBARKATION
Serves units embarking
for overseas duty

Army
Service Forces

1st SERVICE COMMAND
Administers
New England

2nd SERVICE COMMAND
Administers
New York, New Jersey

3rd SERVICE COMMAND
Administers Middle
Atlantic States

4th SERVICE COMMAND
Administers
southeastern U.S.

5th SERVICE COMMAND
Administers Kentucky, Ohio,
Indiana, West Virginia

6th SERVICE COMMAND
Administers Michigan,
Illinois, Wisconsin

7th SERVICE COMMAND
Administers North
Central States

**8th SERVICE
COMMAND**
Administers So
Central State

**9th SERVICE
COMMAND**
Administers
Far West

**NORTHWEST SERVICE
COMMAND**
Administers Alcan Highway
and Alaskan supply route

**MILITARY DISTRICT
OF WASHINGTON**
Under ASF for supply and
administrative functions

**ASF TRAINING
CENTER UNITS**
Train ASF personnel

**ARMY SPECIALIZED
TRAINING PROGRAM**
Trains men in colleges

**ARMY SPECIALIZED TRAINING
PROGRAM RESERVE**
For 17-year-olds

Departments

ANTILLES DEPARTMENT
Controls units in
western Caribbean

ALASKAN DEPARTMENT
Controls units on
Alaskan mainland

**PANAMA CANAL
DEPARTMENT**
Controls units in Canal Zone

**HAWAIIAN
DEPARTMENT**
Controls units in Hawaii

**1st SPECIAL
SERVICE FORCE**
U.S.-Canadian
commando unit

U.S. MILITARY ACADEMY
Army personnel
attached to West Point

Special
Insignia

**ALLIED FORCE
HEADQUARTERS**
Allied staff in North African invasion

COMBAT TEAM 442
Japanese-Americans
attached to the Fifth
Army in Italy

TANK DESTROYER UNITS
Attached to all Ground
Force divisions

**PERSIAN GULF
SERVICE COMMAND**
Moved Lend-Lease supplies to Russia

RANGERS
Specially trained battalions which
fought in Italy and France

**ARMY PERSONNEL
AMPHIBIOUS**
Assigned to Amphibian Units

ARMY PERSONNEL
Assigned to Veterans
Administration

SHAEF
Supreme Headquarters, Allied
Expeditionary Force

Badges of Courage

In August of 1945, "Life" magazine displayed a full roster of arm
patches proudly worn by the men of all America's major military outfits. With the insignia,
"Life" ran a capsule history—reprinted here—of each one's background or war role.

SIXTH ARMY GROUP
Consisted of U.S. Seventh
and French First Armies

TWELFTH ARMY GROUP
Made up of U.S. First, Third,
Ninth, Fifteenth Armies

FIFTEENTH ARMY GROUP
Made up of U.S. Fifth and
British Eighth Armies

FIRST ARMY
Fought in Normandy, took
Paris, first to cross Rhine

SECOND ARMY
Not yet in action, remains
under Army Ground Forces

THIRD ARMY
Exploited Normandy
breakthrough, fought
in France, Germany

FOURTH ARMY
Like the Second Army,
it has not seen action

FIFTH ARMY
Landed at Salerno, took
Rome and rest of Italy

SIXTH ARMY
Fought in New Guinea, invaded
Philippines, took Manila

SEVENTH ARMY
Invaded Sicily, southern France,
fought up Rhône, took Munich

EIGHTH ARMY
Fought in New Guinea, invaded
Philippines, took Mindanao

NINTH ARMY
Captured Brest, Aachen,
northern Ruhr and reached the Elbe

TENTH ARMY
Saw its first action in the
bloody battle of Okinawa

FIFTEENTH ARMY
It is the Army of Occupation
for the U.S. zone in Germany

Corps

I CORPS
Landed on Luzon
with Sixth Army

II CORPS
Fought in North Africa,
joined Fifth Army in Italy

III CORPS
With First Army.
Fought in Ruhr

IV CORPS
With Fifth Army. Its
elements took Rome

V CORPS
Helped take Cherbourg.
Fought across Europe

VI CORPS
Fought in Sicily, Italy,
France, Germany

VII CORPS
Aided V Corps on Cherbourg
peninsula, fought in Germany

VIII CORPS
Brest, Belgian Bulge, Leipzig,
Elbe bridgehead

IX CORPS
To date,
unannounced

X CORPS
With Sixth Army
on Leyte

XI CORPS
With Eighth Army
in Philippines

XII CORPS
With Third Army
at Metz, in Saar

XIII CORPS
With the Ninth Army
across Germany

XIV CORPS
Solomon Islands
and Philippines

XV CORPS
With Seventh Army in
the Vosges Mountains

XVI CORPS
With Ninth Army
in Ruhr, at Essen

XVIII AIRBORNE CORPS
Jumped into Normandy on
D-Day, jumped into Germany

XIX CORPS
Fought across the Rhine,
helped seal off Ruhr pocket

XXI CORPS
Fought in Sicily and Anzio,
invaded southern France

XXII CORPS
Occupation force
in Germany

XXIII CORPS
Occupation force
in Germany

XXIV CORPS
With Sixth Army in Philippines,
with Tenth Army on Okinawa

XX CORPS
Spearheaded Third Army
drive across France

XXXVI CORPS
To date,
unannounced

Defense and Base Commands

ATLANTIC BASE COMMANDS
Under Eastern Defense
Command

**EASTERN DEFENSE
COMMAND**
All U.S. except
Far West

**ANTIAIRCRAFT ARTILLERY COMMAND,
WESTERN DEFENSE
COMMAND**

**ANTIAIRCRAFT ARTILLERY
COMMAND, EASTERN
DEFENSE
COMMAND**

**ICELAND BASE
COMMAND**
Administers Iceland

**GREENLAND BASE
COMMAND**
Administers Greenland

**BERMUDA BASE
COMMAND**
Administers Bermuda

**LABRADOR, NORTHEAST
AND CENTRAL
CANADA COMMAND**

**CARIBBEAN
DEFENSE COMMAND**
Defends Caribbean

Theaters

**EUROPEAN THEATER
OF OPERATIONS**

**U.S. ARMY FORCES
SOUTH ATLANTIC**

**HEADQUARTERS SOUTHEAST
ASIA COMMAND**

**CHINA-BURMA-
INDIA THEATER**

**U.S. ARMY FORCES
PACIFIC OCEAN AREA**

**U.S. ARMY FORCES
IN MIDDLE EAST**

**NORTH AFRICAN
THEATER OF OPERATIONS**

Cavalry Divisions

"PATHFINDER"
ittany, Düren,
ologne plain

9th
El Guettar, Bizerte, Sicily,
Cotentin Peninsula, Germany

10th MOUNTAIN
Arno River, Po Valley

11th AIRBORNE
Leyte, Manila, Cavite

13th AIRBORNE
To date, unannounced

17th AIRBORNE
Parachuted across
Rhine

24th "VICTORY"
New Guinea, Leyte, Corregidor,
Verde Island, Mindanao

32nd "RED ARROW"
Buna, Aitape in
New Guinea, Leyte

33rd "PRAIRIE"
Baguio in northern
Luzon

34th "RED BULL"
Tunisia, Cassino,
Leghorn, Bologna

35th "SANTA FE"
Metz, Nancy,
Ardennes, Ruhr

36th "TEXAS"
Salerno, Cassino,
France, Germany

37th "BUCKEYE"
Munda, Bougainville,
Lingayen Gulf, Manila

38th "CYCLONE"
The recapture of
Bataan

**63rd "BLOOD
AND FIRE"**
Bavaria, Danube River

65th
Saarlautern, Regens-
burg, Danube River

66th "BLACK PANTHER"
Lorient, St. Nazaire,
Army of Occupation

69th
First to link up with
Russians in Germany

70th "TRAILBLAZERS"
Saarbrücken, Moselle
River

71st
Hardt Mountains,
southern Germany

75th
Battle of the Ardennes
Bulge, Westphalia

83rd "OHIO"
Italy, France,
sseldorf, Magdeburg

84th "RAILSPLITTERS"
Ardennes, Hanover

85th "CUSTER"
Rome, Po Valley

86th "BLACK HAWK"
Dachau, Ingolstadt,
southern Germany

87th "ACORN"
Ardennes, Germany,
Czech border

88th "BLUE DEVIL"
Liri Valley, Volterra,
northern Italy

89th "MIDDLE WEST"
Bingen, Eisenach,
central Germany

97th
ntral Germany,
Neumarkt

98th
To date, unannounced

99th
Ardennes, Remagen
bridgehead

100th
Bitche, Remagen
bridgehead, Saar

**101st AIRBORNE
"SCREAMING EAGLE"**
Normandy invasion, Bastogne

102nd "OZARK"
Siegfried Line, Ruhr,
München-Gladbach

103rd
Wissembourg,
Stuttgart, Austria

24th CAVALRY
Inactivated

61st CAVALRY
Inactivated

62nd CAVALRY
Inactivated

63rd CAVALRY
Inactivated

64th CAVALRY
Inactivated

65th CAVALRY
Inactivated

66th CAVALRY
Inactivated

1st
Tunisia, Sicily, Normandy,
the Bulge, Germany

2nd "INDIAN HEAD"
Normandy,
the Ardennes,
Leipzig

3rd "MARNE"
Sicily, Cassino, Anzio,
Colmar pocket, Munich

4th "IVY"
Cherbourg, Bastogne

5th "RED DIAMOND"
Metz, Luxembourg, Mainz-
Worms bridgehead

6th
Sansapor in New Guinea,
northern Luzon

7th "SIGHT-SEEING"
Attu, Kwajalein,
Leyte, Okinawa

8th

25th "TROPIC LIGHTNING"
Guadalcanal, New
Georgia, Philippines

26th "YANKEE"
Battle of the Bulge,
Siegfried Line

27th "NEW YORK"
Makin Island, Saipan,
Okinawa

28th "KEYSTONE"
Paris, Hürtgen Forest,
Colmar pocket

29th "BLUE AND GRAY"
D-Day in Normandy,
Siegfried Line, Aachen

30th "OLD HICKORY"
St. Lô, Aachen, Malmédy,
Stavelot, Rhine crossing

31st "DIXIE"
Davao in southe...
Mindanao

39th
Inactivated

40th "SUNSHINE"
Los Negros, Luzon, Panay
Island in Philippines

41st "SUNSET"
Salamaua, Marshalls,
Mindanao, Palawan

42nd "RAINBOW"
Schweinfurt, Munich,
Dachau

43rd "RED WING"
New Georgia, New
Guinea, Luzon

44th
The Saar, Ulm,
Danube River

45th "THUNDERBIR...
Sicily, Salerno, Cass...
Anzio, Belfort Gap

76th
Luxembourg, Germany

77th "STATUE OF LIBERTY"
Guam, Leyte, Okinawa

78th "LIGHTNING"
Aachen, Roer River
and the Ruhr

79th "LORRAINE"
D-Day, Normandy break-
through, Vosges Mountains

80th "BLUE RIDGE"
Normandy, Moselle River,
relief of Bastogne

81st "WILDCAT"
Angaur, Peleliu
and Ulithi

82nd AIRBORNE "ALL AMERICAN"
Sicily, Normandy,
Nijmegen, Ardennes

D...

90th "TOUGH 'OMBRES"
Normandy, Metz,
Czechoslovakia

91st "WILD WEST"
Arno River, Pisa,
Bologna

92nd "BUFFALO"
Arno River, Po
Valley, Genoa

93rd
Bougainville

94th
Brittany, Siegfried Line,
Moselle River, Saar

95th
Metz, Moselle River,
Siegfried Line, Saar

96th
Leyte, Okinawa

C...

104th "TIMBER WOLF"
Rhine crossing,
Cologne, Ruhr

106th
St. Vith, Battle of
the Bulge

AMERICAL
Guadalcanal, Bougainville,
Cebu Island in Philippines

1st CAVALRY "HELL FOR LEATHER"
Los Negros, Leyte, Manila

2nd CAVALRY
Inactivated

3rd CAVALRY
Inactivated

Our Heroes: Joe Foss

Reacting to their early defeats, Americans hailed a handful of heroes with special fervor. Among the proudest tributes to these fighting men was a series in *Esquire* magazine, devoted mainly to winners of the nation's highest award for bravery, the Congressional Medal of Honor. Their deeds, recounted in impassioned prose by novelist and former sports writer Paul Gallico, stirred millions of readers; the illustrations by John Falter were cut out and pinned up on thousands of kids' walls and in high-school homerooms. The articles, four of which are excerpted on these pages, told of men who differed greatly. But all of them fit Gallico's homey description of the famed Marine aviator Joe Foss: "He was just a plain American guy with a sense of responsibility to the rest of the gang."

Captain Joe Foss of the United States Marines, ranking American ace with a score of 26 Japanese planes shot down, tying the record Captain Eddie Rickenbacker made in World War I, was awarded the Congressional Medal of Honor for outstanding heroism and achievement. Joe Foss's place in the Esquire Hall of Heroes is awarded him for the Zeroes he did not shoot down to break Rick's record. Tough Joe, the Dakota farm boy turned flier, won in a gigantic poker game of pure bluff where you held a fist full of nothing and made the other guy lose his nerve.

It was Joe's last week on Guadalcanal. The Japs came over, 40 Zeroes in formation, screening a huge flight of bombers, more than 30 of them. The bombers would smash Henderson Field and its vital installations once and for all. Joe took his hand upstairs to play out the game. Foss lined up his eight Grummans and posted his four P-38s above them.

The Japs threw out bait, expendables who wanted the little flight of Grummans to break formation and dog-fight. Then superior numbers would wipe them out. Zeroes presented themselves in inviting attitudes. Foss wouldn't even look at them. The slugs in his web belts were being saved up for the big boys hanging back with their load of destruction.

The Zeroes grew more daring. One of them practically slid down Joe Foss's gun barrel, asking for it. Foss flipped his ship aside. The temptation to become that super-ace must have been enormous. But the backfield was carrying the ball. One of the Lightnings screamed down from above and made the Jap another name on the family scroll of honored dead.

Three more times the Japs tried Foss and three more Japs were shot down by the backfield Lockheeds. Foss kept his formation, smiling his impudent smile behind the chewed cigar butt.

Joe Foss and all of the pilots up there that steaming January afternoon were dead men if the Jap chose to throw in his entire force, and they knew it. Their nerves must have screamed to shoot it out. Foss held them in.

The bluff was beginning to work. The Jap was beginning to wonder if he did hold the winning hand. Precious gasoline was burning away in his cylinder heads. The big bombers were lapping it up. They all had a long way to go home.

And the Jap threw in the hand. He turned and flew home without dropping a bomb, or scoring a hit on an American ship.

Joe Foss and his little team dropped down onto Henderson Field. Foss still had his 26 Zeroes and his tie with Eddie Rickenbacker. But he was a bigger hero than he had ever been.

David Waybur

As Gallico tells it, Lieutenant David Waybur reenacted the David and Goliath story near Agrigento, Sicily, during the Allied invasion of 1943. The American David was a 150-pound former ranch hand from Piedmont, California. The new Goliath was a 12-ton Italian tank—followed by three more just like it. The tank wounded David and half of his six-man patrol, then moved in for the kill.

In the moonlight a lone figure, a tiny figure opposed to the huge, looming, fire-spitting black bulks of the tanks, stood in the roadway, one hand holding his wounded side, the other cradling a .45 caliber Thompson sub-machinegun. His men were scattered in the ditch, bleeding from wounds, taking cover where they could behind the riddled jeeps and in clumps of cactus; but David stood uncovered and unprotected, facing the Fascist giant.

As young David of Bethlehem slung his stone, so David of Piedmont loosed a burst from his pitiable popgun and hit Goliath squarely between the eyes and slew him. The slugs went ripping through the open ports of the tank, killing the crew. Insensate then, the mechanical monster ground on straight ahead onto the shattered bridge to fall with a dreadful iron clangor into the stream bed below.

The three monsters following paused to think it over. Lieutenant Waybur, disabled now by the wound in his hip, toppled into the ditch. But the tanks had had enough. Overestimating the strength of the defenders, they contented themselves with firing all night into the cactus cover.

Waybur gave his pistol to Private First Class Ball of Eureka Springs, Arkansas, and sent him for help. Ball got through. In the morning he brought supporting vehicles, infantry and medical corps men. The enemy abandoned the three tanks and fled, leaving them to be captured intact by the Americans.

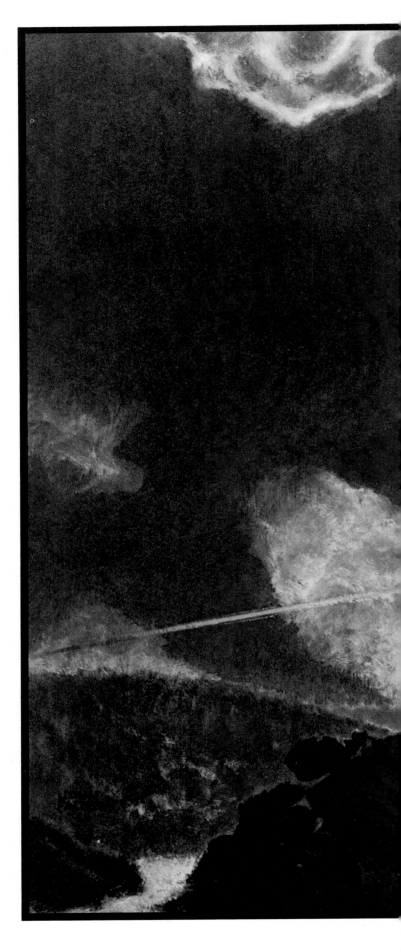

Reinhardt J. Keppler

Reinhardt J. Keppler had a special motive for patriotic devotion: his father had come to America seeking the freedom denied him in Germany. Reinhardt enlisted in the Navy at 18; he was a Boatswain's Mate First Class aboard the U.S.S. *San Francisco* when that heavy cruiser joined the battle of Savo Island in November 1942. Suddenly, fire threatened his ship's store of explosives.

It was Boatswain's Mate First Class Keppler, charged with fire fighting, who went to the rescue of his ship. Single-handed he led a hose into the blazing area and fought the fire alone. One stubborn kid, ringed by flame. Choking smoke, fumes and rivers of running fire faced him. Behind him, the enemy shells roaring out of the darkness crashed through the steel skin of the ship and blew up into deadly fragments.

Keppler brought the fire under control. The dreaded explosion never took place.

Fifteen major caliber shells struck the "San Francisco" and sprayed the night with splinters of shredding steel. Some of those splinters tore into the person of Reinhardt Keppler and killed him. The boy might not have died, would not have died, if he had gone to a dressing station for help. But there were fires again reaching for the vitals of the ship, and all about him were the cries and moans of the other wounded.

No longer able to lug his lengths of hose into the inferno of flame, he directed the fire-fighting operations, coolly and efficiently. And to the wounded lying on all sides of him, he brought the help that he himself disdained, first aid, bandages, tourniquets. With each move, the heart within him that beat with pity and love was pumping his own life away, until there was no more to sustain love, or life. Many brave men have died in this war. This was the manner of passing of Reinhardt Keppler.

Howard W. Gilmore

The submarine *Growler*, skippered by twice-decorated Commander Howard W. Gilmore, was caught on the surface on February 7, 1943, by a Japanese gunboat. Moving fast, Gilmore succeeded in ramming the gunboat and crippling it. As the sub made ready to crash-dive, the Japanese sailors leaped to their guns. Gilmore, standing on the submarine's bridge, was hit badly by a machine-gun burst.

The men came clambering out the hatch to pick up Gilmore. On the deck of the sinking gunboat, a Jap crew was working desperately to bring a three-incher to bear on the sub. The commander ordered: "All hands below!"

The order was obeyed. It had to be obeyed. Only the officer of the deck remained topside, struggling to lift his fallen commander. The distance between the sub and the enemy gunboat was increasing. In another moment, the heavy cannon could be brought to bear. The skipper gave his last command: "Take her down!"

The deck officer scrambled down the conning tower. The hatch cover slammed shut with an iron clang, echoed by the bullets ringing from its side. On the gunboat the three-incher spanged sharply. The projectile yelled as it passed over the diving submarine and tore a spume from the surface of the sea beyond. Only the top of the conning tower was visible now, with the wounded officer still clinging to it.

In a swirl of white, salt froth, the submarine vanished beneath the surface. The commander died alone in the sea. Many weeks later, the submarine came home.

When Commander Gilmore gave his last order, he knew that he was going to die, that there was no hope of survival. He signed his own death warrant to save his ship and crew. Over the scream of flying metal, the crash of exploding cordite and the hissing of the sea, rang his magnificent cry—"Take her down!"

First Lieutenant Audie Murphy obligingly displays two of his medals: the coveted Congressional Medal of Honor (left) and the Legion of Merit.

The Mostest Hero

Farmersville, Texas—population 2,206—turned out en masse on June 15, 1945, to welcome home Lieutenant Audie Murphy, recently returned from the battlefields of North Africa, Italy and France. A basically modest man, he listened with embarrassment as one dignitary after another lauded his combat record and dramatically recounted the heroic feat that won him the Congressional Medal of Honor with the citation quoted below. Yet the Farmersville reception touched Audie deeply. The mayor's speech was matched in generosity by the gifts of the townspeople, who remembered Audie's hard times as the orphaned boy of sharecroppers. Murphy had a tear in his eye as he thanked his friends and then sent them home: "I know you people don't want to stand in this hot sun any longer and just look at me."

For Audie, peacetime brought no respite from public adulation, or from the lingering shocks of war. Constantly restless and dissatisfied, he took off for Hollywood and there began writing his war memoirs. The book, entitled

To Hell and Back was published in 1949, and although it enjoyed brisk sales, Audie was far from pleased with it. "Even though I tried to tell the exact truth," he said, "it came out more than life size." While writing the book, he also tried his hand in the movies, but was damned with faint praise for his acting. Through his work in the studios, he met and married actress Wanda Hendrix, but their much-publicized marriage soon ended in divorce. Through it all, Murphy could not forget his debt to the service: "I have to admit I love the damned Army, it was father, mother, brother to me."

But Audie tried valiantly to lay the ghost of the war. He even gave away his medals *(overleaf)* to children of relatives, and for those who considered this disrespectful, Audie repeatedly explained that it was just the opposite, and his remarks revealed a man who was profoundly and permanently a soldier. "I didn't feel that they entirely belonged to me," he said. "My whole unit earned them, but I didn't know how to give them to the whole unit."

Second Lieutenant Audie L. Murphy, 15th Infantry, 3rd Division, 26 January 1945, near Holtzwihr, France, commanded Company B, which was attacked by six tanks and waves of infantry. Lieutenant Murphy ordered his men to withdraw to prepared positions in a woods, while he remained forward at his command post and continued to give fire directions to the artillery by telephone. Behind him, to his right, one of our tank destroyers received a direct hit and began to burn. Its crew withdrew to the woods. Lieutenant Murphy continued to direct artillery fire which killed large numbers of the advancing enemy infantry. With the enemy tanks abreast of his position, Lieutenant Murphy climbed on the burning tank destroyer, which was in danger of blowing up at any moment, and employed its .50 caliber machine gun against the enemy. He was alone and exposed to German fire from three sides, but his deadly fire killed dozens of Germans *and caused their infantry attack to waver. The enemy tanks, losing infantry support, began to fall back. For an hour the Germans tried every available weapon to eliminate Lieutenant Murphy, but he continued to hold his position and wiped out a squad which was trying to creep up unnoticed on his right flank. Germans reached as close as ten yards, only to be mowed down by his fire. He received a leg wound, but ignored it and continued the single-handed fight until his ammunition was exhausted. He then made his way to his company, refused medical attention, and organized the company in a counterattack ... His directing of artillery fire wiped out many of the enemy; he killed or wounded about 50. Lieutenant Murphy's indomitable courage and his refusal to give an inch of ground saved his company from possible encirclement and destruction, and enabled it to hold the woods which had been the enemy's objective.*

117

Audie's Medals

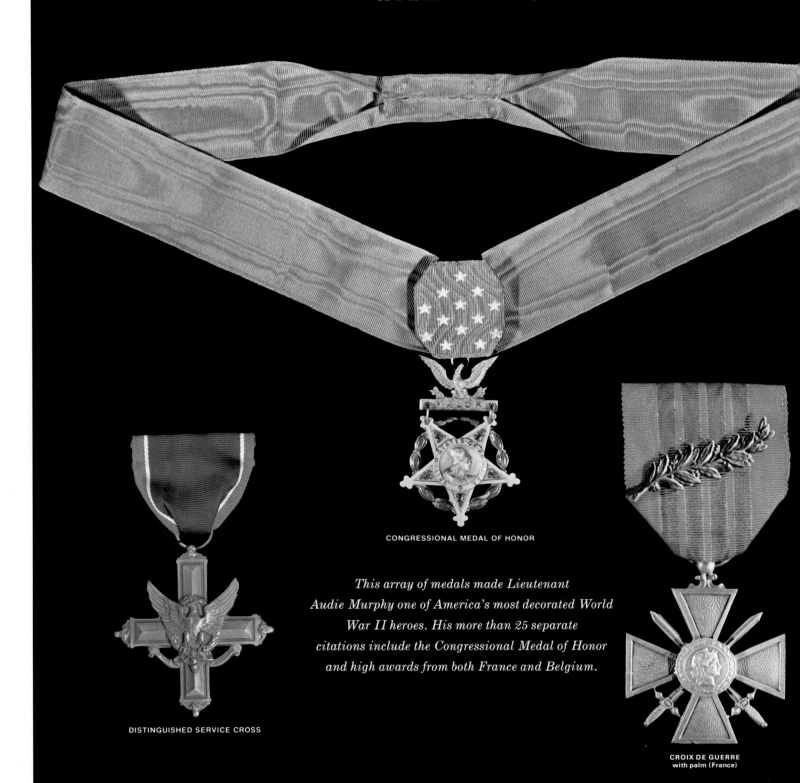

CONGRESSIONAL MEDAL OF HONOR

DISTINGUISHED SERVICE CROSS

CROIX DE GUERRE
with palm (France)

*This array of medals made Lieutenant
Audie Murphy one of America's most decorated World
War II heroes. His more than 25 separate
citations include the Congressional Medal of Honor
and high awards from both France and Belgium.*

PURPLE HEART.
with oak leaf clusters

SILVER STAR.
with oak leaf cluster

VICTORY MEDAL

EUROPEAN. AFRICAN
AND
MIDDLE EASTERN
CAMPAIGN MEDAL

BRONZE STAR
for valor, with oak leaf cluster

AMERICAN CAMPAIGN
MEDAL

LEGION OF MERIT

GOOD CONDUCT MEDAL

CROIX DE GUERRE.
with palm (Belgium)

At Ease

For every serviceman sent into the line on combat duty, many others drew robot chores in the rear: sorting ships' stores in Norfolk, Virginia, or unloading endless supplies onto the damp docks of Southampton, England; manning airfields in dismal holes like Ascension Island or churning out reams of tedious official documents from a desk in Tunis. Even for those in the combat area, the brief hours of terror under fire were interspersed with days, weeks, even months of doing nothing in some of the dreariest places on earth.

The ennui had some strange effects. One shorebound Navy man, standing his umpteenth midnight watch in a Melanesian swamp hundreds of miles from the enemy, shot up a line of laundry, later testifying that an unidentified moving object had failed to give the password. Said another man, stationed in the boondocks outside Darwin, Australia, "Listen, buddy, here's how it is. After a while you find yourself talking to yourself. Then you find yourself talking to the lizards. Then you find the lizards talking to you. And pretty soon you find yourself listening." In other theaters, the men behind the lines took on the ultimate enemy, monotony, in the simple ways shown on the following pages.

A marble trophy from Anzio, Italy, stands garbed in a regulation tin hat.

Nothing Like a Dame

Though the American military was notorious for supplying its men with the mostest and bestest of materiel *(page 173),* nothing in any U.S. regulation manual provided for the one item that seemed most necessary for a man's well-being. "What ain't we got?" asked the chorus of island-bound gobs in Rodgers and Hammerstein's musical *South Pacific.* The answer, of course: "We ain't got dames."

Lacking the live article, soldiers substituted pinups. They plastered the doors of their lockers, the walls of their Quonset huts, even the insides of their helmet liners with girlie pictures. Among the favorites were a photograph of Rita Hayworth in a nightgown and one of Betty Grable in a bathing suit *(pages 124-125).* Almost as popular were the sultry paintings of girls dressed in diaphanous costumes that appeared each month in *Esquire.* So sexy were these ladies that in 1944 Postmaster General Frank C. Walker banned them from the mails, thus earning the everlasting fury of every GI pinup fan.

We would like to know who in hell got the bright idea of banning pictures from your most popular "Esquire." After all those men in Africa, the Aleutians, Italy, etc., have done for those so-called spiritually minded human beings back in the States, they should have consideration to a certain extent about this matter.

You won't find one barracks overseas that hasn't got an Esquire Pin-Up Girl. I, for one, have close to fifteen of them, and none of them seems to demoralize me in the least. Those pictures are very much on the clean and healthy side and it gives us guys a good idea of what we're fighting for. What will these ignorant specimens think up next? Maybe ban the sending of cigarettes to the men because they stimulate nicotine poison? I wish these high-browed monkeys could spend a year overseas without anything but magazines.

LEE J. MAHONEY F 2/C

BERNARD L. McKINNON F 2/C

ALBERT J. FRANCO S 1/C

Their Quonset hut papered with pinups, airmen in the Aleutians play cards. Besides looking good, the girlie photos helped keep out the cold.

Rita Hayworth

Betty Grable

At a makeshift laundromat in a tropical river, leathernecks on Guadalcanal use a fallen tree to scrub the jungle dirt out of their battle fatigues.

The Joys of Housekeeping

Lack of love was not the only drawback to the all-male military world. What hurt almost as much was doing all the housekeeping chores that in civilian life were pushed off on women. At sea, sailors seemed to spend half their time mopping and the rest handscrubbing their laundry.

Soldiers, too, were forced to become their own laundresses, seamstresses and general homemakers. Even in combat zones, veteran infantrymen would indulge in rudimentary interior decorating to make their foxholes more livable, building roofs out of tree limbs and lining the walls and floors with empty shell casings.

The most thoroughly despised of all the military housekeeping chores was Kitchen Police, which was both humiliating—in theory, only privates and goof-offs pulled it—and tough. It began before dawn and ended after dark, and consisted of massive bouts of dishwashing, scrubbing of garbage cans and the lugging of enormous quantities of food from storage depots to stoveside. Worse yet, once the food got into the hands of Army cooks, all the prior sweat of fetching and toting rarely seemed worth the effort. The crowning irony was that despite centuries of conclusive evidence to the contrary, the Army officially considered its cookery *haute cuisine*—as evidenced by the following passage from a training manual for cooks.

There is no limit to what can be done to improve a mess by thought and care and seasoning, attractive serving, and inventing new combinations and mixtures of foods. The pleasant task of cooking becomes doubly interesting to the cook who is not satisfied with merely cooking well, but takes advantage of every opportunity of finding new and pleasant ways to prepare food. To him, cooking is not just a task—it is a pleasure.

Good cooking is recognized the world over as a fine art, and a good cook commands respect. Cooks who perfect themselves in their art are always in demand, and many have acquired wealth and fame. TRAINING MANUAL 10-405 *THE ARMY COOK*

An irate mess sergeant posts a comment about rations on his mess hall.

"Learn a trade in the Army," ran one recruiting slogan. Many GIs did.

Motherly and terribly proper in her neatly tailored uniform, an English Red Cross lady hands out coffee and donuts to a GI and his captain.

Barefoot and topless, a cheerful coterie of Melanesian ladies brings aid and comfort to the crew of a B-17 bomber forced down on New Guinea.

Mail Call

Most servicemen's only contacts with home were through the letters and magazines that arrived at mail call. For men so hungry for reading matter that they would spend hours poring over the fine print on K-ration boxes, the mailbag produced treasured reminders that somewhere there was still a world of clean sheets, edible food, no duty and women. An Air Force sergeant wrote *Yank* magazine, "You can find soldiers carrying around letters so rubbed, worn and crumpled from hikes and work and general wear that they can only be read from memory. But we hold onto them." The ones they held the longest were "sugar reports" from girl friends, but any old letter would do. Millions were sent, and millions written in reply by the GIs—so many, in fact, that to save shipping space the War Department devised a miniaturized letter form known as V-mail *(below, left).*

Every line of every kind of mail was read by a censor, who was likely to cut half the news that a serviceman wanted to give or receive. However, most veterans found ways to frustrate the censor by devising intricate family codes to pass on important tidbits. One housewife began packing whenever her Navy husband described a certain kind of seabird; the real message: his ship was due in for refitting. But the soldier who really brought the censor to his knees did so by accident—as reported by Sergeant Eugene Drucker, whose letter is among the samples at right.

I am sending you a clipping on our raid on Naples Harbour, Feb. 7. It was probably in the papers in the states but I clipped this out of the Egyptian Gazette.

Everything is fine with me, however I would sure love to get home if only for a short time, as I have been away for over a year. I am getting used to this desert life and living in a tent, and we are suffering no real hardship.

I have about 200 hours of combat time in the air in B24s which is heavy bombardment and one does get a little tired of it after a time. Even though you do get used to being shot at it does wear on a person. . . . LIEUTENANT DELBERT HALL, NORTH AFRICA, 1943

You remember the Palmer boy, who is stationed here. Well, he was up town and ran into Sgt. Arlo Fox from Spirit Lake, so he brought Arlo and his two friends down to the hospital and when I met him I remarked how sorry I was about his mother's death, and that was his first knowledge of her death in March. . . . Arlo spent the night with me and I tried to console him, but he took it mighty hard. . . . CAPTAIN DON RODAWIG, NORTH AFRICA, 1943

We have been fighting in the woods of Germany for some while now, living in fox holes and cooking our K-rations on small paper fires. The K-rations come packed in an oil-covered carton which will just about heat a canteen cup of water for your morning coffee, and believe me it certainly tastes good. But I think I'd give anything for a glass of milk and a hot meal.

While we were in France everyone was so glad to see us. They threw flowers in our path and gave us wine and fruit. All the girls kissed the soldiers, which is the French way of saying they are glad to see you—nice way, don't you think. However, in Germany there are no flowers, fruit or kisses for the Yankees and you have to watch everyone . . .

CAPTAIN MERWIN TOLLES, SOMEWHERE IN GERMANY, 1944

I thought I had been doing pretty well as far as letter-writing went, but one of the OSS guards has me beat. He claims to have written 2,827 letters (including V-mails) in his one year away from the States, and he gives no sign of slackening. To his wife he never writes less than three letters a day, and he told me that once, "just for the helluvit," he wrote her nine letters during one 12-hour guard period. I asked him how his wife took this prodigious effort and he replied: "For a while she thought it was cute but now she says she ain't got no place to keep them. She's got her bureau all full and then she started throwing them in the closet, but now she says they're leaking out." I asked him, incidentally, if he didn't think he was placing an undue strain on the censor and the mails. He thought for a moment, then replied, "Well, Jeez, it's my morale ain't it?"

In London, the poor and conscientious lieutenant who had to censor this astounding production would come in early in the morning and demand angrily, "Well, how many did you write last night?" As time went on the lieutenant became more and more upset, and on several occasions had to alter his plans for the evening in order not to get behind. One day he got very sore and barged out of his office and up to the guard desk yelling "God dammit Zicceli. I'm getting fed up with reading your goddam stupid letters! Why don't you die and dry up? I hate you and I hate your goddam wife and I hate your butcher and all the other bastards you maintain that constant diarrhea with."

According to Zicceli, the lieutenant threatened to get him transferred. Finally he WAS transferred, to Paris. Several days later, who should walk in but the lieutenant himself—transferred too. He took one look at Zicceli and groaned, "Oh my God!"

SERGEANT EUGENE P. DRUCKER, PARIS, 1944

Since seeing you in England I have sort of covered three more countries: France, Germany and Austria. I've seen what wasn't ever meant for human eyes to see. We were in Landsberg—Hitler's prison cell where he wrote "Mein Kampf." Dachau was close by. Have you ever seen stacks and piles of HUMAN bodies—200 to 300 in each pile, sprawled out, starved and beaten and gassed to death?

The only thing I've seen to compare with it was at the Landsberg camp. The evening before we moved in they had put 250 people, men and women, into this house which was sort of half dug in. The house was then saturated with gasoline and a match was all that was necessary.

The next morning we moved in under a hazy cloud of smoke. But it didn't smell like ordinary smoke. Have you ever smelled human flesh burning? That was it!!! We now have an outfit that cannot smell any sort of fire smoke without that incident and those scenes passing through his mind, because, it seems that it will never leave us, never. . . .

AN ANONYMOUS GI, SOMEWHERE IN GERMANY, 1945

The first Army morale show in Normandy (above and right) was put on by a liberated French troupe, which had once been hired by the Wehrmacht.

Touring Burma with the USO, Ann Sheridan hugs a blissful dogface, who has just given her his most precious souvenir—a bloodied Japanese flag.

Eager GIs cluster around their favorite USO flame—Marlene Dietrich.

Two newly freed French acrobats cavort for Normandy invasion troops.

Greeting his liberators, a French peasant happily offers a sip of victory cheer to a clattering half-track full of GIs on their way to occupy Paris.

In Paris at last, U.S. infantrymen drop their packs to dig into an al fresco feast laid out on a street corner by a party of celebrating townspeople.

The Bitter Edge

The supreme—but unofficial—spokesman for the gripes and prejudices of the Army enlisted man was a puckish GI in his early twenties named Bill Mauldin, who drew cartoons for the Army newspaper *Stars and Stripes.* A round peg in the squared-off atmosphere of military life (during one four-month period he stood 64 days of punitive K.P.), Mauldin aimed irreverent broadsides at every phase of Army life, including top brass and senior N.C.O.s, like the veteran cavalry sergeant opposite who delivers the horseman's traditional *coup de grace* to his disabled jeep.

But Mauldin's most famous cartoons featured two sardonic, battle-grimed dogfaces named Willie and Joe, whose scraggly beards, bleary eyes and dented helmets summed up all the agony of the infantryman's war. As Mauldin followed Willie and Joe's real-life counterparts through the battlefields of Italy and France, his humor took on the bitter edge revealed in the cartoons *(pages 138-139)* and in the excerpt below from his book *Up Front.*

Maybe I can be funny after the war, but nobody who has seen this war can be cute about it while it's going on. The only way I can try to be a little funny is to make something out of the humorous situations which come up even when you don't think life could be any more miserable.

Joe and Willie don't look much like the cream of young American manhood which was sent overseas in the infantry. Neither of them is boyish, although neither is aged. Joe is in his early twenties and Willie is in his thirties—pretty average ages for the infantry. While they are no compliment to young American manhood's good looks, their expressions are those of infantry soldiers who have been in the war for a couple of years.

Look at an infantryman's eyes and you can tell how much war he has seen. Look at his actions in a bar and listen to his talk. If he is cocky and troublesome, and talks about how many battles he's fought, and if he goes around looking for a fight and depending upon his uniform to get him special privileges, then he has not had it. If he is looking very weary and resigned to the fact that he is probably going to die before it is over, and if he has a deep, almost hopeless desire to go home and forget it all; if he looks with dull, uncomprehending eyes at the fresh-faced kid who is talking about the joys of battle and killing Germans, then he comes from the same infantry as Joe and Willie.

Perched on a bombed-out house, Mauldin sketches his view of the war.

Mauldin's favorite cartoon was this one. At first, nobody else liked it much, but he kept resubmitting it until it became a favorite with everyone.

"Ever notice th' funny sound these zippers make, Willie?"

"Aim between th' eyes; Joe . . .
sometimes they charge when they're wounded."

"She must be very purty. Th' whole column is wheezin' at her."

"I'd ruther cover th' gun. I won't hafta dry myself with a oily rag."

'"Now that ya mention it, it does sound like th' patter of rain on a tin roof."

"Don't startle 'im, Joe—it's almost full."

"My son. Five days old. Good-lookin' kid, ain't he?"

V-E Day *"Th' hell with it. I ain't standin' up till he does!"*

A starred flag indicates three men in the service.

The Taxpayers' War

The town was whole. The malted milks still whirled at Bullard's store;
and Oppenheimer-Stern announced their sale of new spring rayons just
as sheer as nylons.   MACKINLAY KANTOR, *THE WAR IN BOONE CITY,* 1943

Every morning for four years, the first thing just about everyone did was to grab the newspaper *(right and overleaf)* to find out who was ahead in the war. It was easy to tell; World War II was, as TIME magazine said, "the best reported war in history." U.S. papers had at least 500 correspondents with the armed forces—five times more than in World War I. These reporters filed half a million words a day and were extraordinarily courageous: they flew in bombers through Berlin flak and rode on landing craft onto Pacific Islands and European beaches.

They did this not only because they were brave, but because the American people had a deep and perhaps guilty curiosity about the war, which was, despite all the thundering slogans, much less than a total war—and far, far away. Between the two fronts—home and battle *(pages 72-139)*—the contrast was enormous. At home, aside from sending sons and husbands off to fight and producing vast quantities of materiel, the war effort was mainly trivia: watching for enemy planes that never came; rationing meat, sugar and gas; trying to make do with a scarcity of hairpins and glass eyes.

Beyond that the war was, in many respects, good to noncombatants. In crucial 1943, for example, the U.S. living standard was one sixth higher than in 1939. A bombardier home on furlough in 1944 said: "Their way of life hasn't really changed a damn bit. One day I was riding on a subway and I heard one bastard say to another one, 'If this war lasts for two more years I'll be on easy street.'"

Business generally prospered, especially big business, which made itself still bigger as it wove complex new ties to the military. By 1945, of all Army and Navy dollar obligations 82 per cent were tightly held by the top 100 corporations. As wartime profits soared to new peaks, so did peacetime prospects: 31 giant companies operated half the government's $18 billion worth of new factories; afterward these companies would buy the plants for a song.

Yet the total effect of all this reached far beyond profiteering and personal pleasure. For ultimately the war was won at home, by the home front. America's guns, generals and GIs were good. But so were the enemies'. Where the U.S. was stunningly unique was in the massive financing and production of armaments *(pages 146-153)*, and in getting these armaments overseas. In 1942 an American officer who was methodically smothering a hill in Tunisia under artillery fire explained it all to a correspondent: "I'm letting the American taxpayer take this hill."

San Francisco Chronicle EXTRA
THE CITY'S ONLY HOME-OWNED NEWSPAPER
FOUNDED 1865—VOL. CLVIII, NO. 112 CCCC SAN FRANCISCO, SATURDAY, MAY 6, 1944 DAILY 5 CENTS, SUNDAY 15 CENTS:

S. F. RATION STAMP RACKET SMASHED

OPA Uncovers Ring

Three Men Are Accused Of Stealing and Selling Gas and Ration Coupons

Bank Employe Is a Suspect; Investigators Declare Sales Were Made to Shipyard Workers

An amazing black market ring in gas coupons and ration stamps, allegedly stolen by trusted workers in a local bank, was smashed yesterday, the O. P. A. declared.

In custody, it was learned, were two Marinship employes—George Kirkham, 25, of Marin City, and Emeio J. Maionchi, 27, of 2205 Jones street, San Francisco.

Shoe coupons also were also allegedly peddled at the shipyard for $1 each. The racket, described as one of the most insidious uncovered by OPA investigators to date, operated in this manner, according to Chief Investigator Roy Danforth:

A suspected clerk of the bank, which handles the consumer-cashed ration stamps turned in by merchants and service station operators, entered the deposits in regular fashion. These gas coupons and the red and blue ration stamps are pasted onto large sheets before depositing.

The suspected clerk, OPA investigators said, after making the ledger entries, steamed off the stamps and coupons, then smuggled them out the rear door.

From that rear door, the course of the stolen stamps into the black market was traced, OPA said, through admissions by Kirkham.

KIRKHAM ARRESTED

Kirkham, they said, acted as a sort of retailer and reputedly admitted peddling some 300 coupons and stamps—gas, read and blue. He was arrested several days ago and released on bond.

Kirkham told investigators he received his illegal stamps from Maionchi, who was described as a "jobber" or intermediary for the bank clerk. Maionchi, it was stated, was picked up in the vicinity of the Marinship yard late yesterday after he had allegedly delivered additional second-hand stamps to Kirkham. He was booked at the County Jail at San Rafael as "en route" to the U. S. Marshal here.

How extensive were the operations of this "inside" ring was not immediately known. Further arrests were expected.

House Passes Simplified Tax Bill

By the Associated Press

WASHINGTON, May 5—**Spurred by the national outcry against the intricacy and confusion of wartime taxation, the** House passed unanimously today a bill designed to relieve some 30,000,000 of the 50,000,000 taxpayers of the necessity of computing income tax returns.

The vote was 358 to 0, the first time in the memory of House veterans that a tax bill passed without a dissenting vote.

This action shuttled the tax simplication legislation to the Senate, where Chairman George (D., Ga.) of the Finance Committee, predicted early approval.

The streamliner would:

1—Scrap the 2-year-old "Victory" tax and set new normal and surtax rates and exemptions while keeping actual tax burdens near present levels.

2—Change the withholding levy against wages and salaries—effective next January 1—to deduct currently the full tax liability of persons earning up to $5000—thus removing the necessity for 30,000,000 persons to compute formal returns.

3—Of the 20,000,000 who still would be required to file returns, 10,000,000 (those earning less than $5000 but with income other than wages and salaries(could use a simple table showing their entire tax. The remaining 10,000,000, with incomes over $5000, would fill out a simpler return than the present long form

SINGLE PERSONS

The revised normal and surtaxes would be applicable for returns filed next March 15 on 1944 income.

Generally the bill would levy a somewhat larger tax against single persons and couples without children, while the load would be light-

Continued on Page 4, Col. 6

The Axis Arms

Third article in the series by Nat A. Barrows on the Axis invasion preparations will be printed in Sunday's paper.

British Face Tighter Rationing

WASHINGTON, May 5 (AP)—Great Britain, in contrast to recent developments here, is preparing for a possible tightening of food rationing and a continuation of controls for possibly two years after the war in Europe ends.

James A. Scott Watson, retiring British agricultural attache in this country, told a press conference this today, adding that his country saw little hope of normal food supplies before 1947. He ascribed a sharp difference in meat supplies of the two countries largely to the necessity of using United Nations shipping for movement of war materials and fighting men.

(AP) Wirephoto

ADMIRAL SOEMU TOYODA
He succeeds Koga as Japanese fleet commander

Drive Toward Tokyo

U. S. Planes Hit Jap Air Bases In New Guinea

By the Associated Press

ADVANCED ALLIED H. Q., Southwest Pacific, Saturday, May 6 (AP)—Allied planes have intensified their campaign on neutralizing the Schouten islands in Dutch New Guinea area where the Japanese are reported massing naval air strength, headquarters announced today.

Several enemy planes were smashed on the ground, and interceptors were driven off in a new raid on Schouten airbases which lie more than 200 miles northwest of invaded Hollandia.

That is in the sector where a spokesman said yesterday the Japanese were sending reinforcements of their well-trained naval flyers to block the westward movement of General Douglas MacArthur's forces toward the Philippines.

WEWAK HIT AGAIN

Wake island air base, the nearest one to the West of Hollandia, also was raided and neutralizing attacks were continued against Wewak to the southeast of Hollandia.

Some of the estimated 60,000 Japanese troops isolated between Hollandia and the Madang area have been noticed concentrating at Wewak.

In the Wewak-Hansa bay sector where the Nipponese have been trying to flee on barges, headquarters reported today that swift patrol torpedo boats had damaged 20 more barges and silenced three shore batteries.

Wandering groups of starving, dejected Japanese are continuing to give themselves up to the Hollandia invasion forces. A spokesman said today the total number of the enemy which has surrendered there now totals 155. Although small, that is large when contrasted with other similar operations of the past. Here-

Continued on Page 4, Col. 2

Japs' Naval Chief Koga Dies in Action

By the Associated Press

WASHINGTON, May 5—Admiral Mineichi Koga, commander of the combined Japanese fleet, was killed in action on an undisclosed front in March—the second Japanese fleet chief to die in action within a year—and has been succeeded by the colorless Admiral Soemu Toyoda, the Tokyo High Command announced today.

An imperial headquarters communique recorded by U. S. Government monitors said Koga had "died at his post in March of this year while directing operations from an airplane at the front."

It bore a striking similarity to the Tokyo communique of May 21, 1943, announcing the death of the former fleet chief, boastful Isoroku Yamamoto, in a warplane the previous April.

NO DETAILS GIVEN

Yamamoto, who once boasted he would dictate the peace terms in the White House, was known as the man who torpedoed the London naval conference in 1934 and planned the attack on Pearl Harbor. Tokyo indicated last year that he died a spectacular death

Continued on Page 3, Col. 2

Hitler Calls in Group of Envoys

LONDON, May 5 (AP)—Adolf Hitler has called to his headquarters the German envoys in neutral capitals, the Moscow radio said today. Franz von Papen already is home from Turkey, which has cut off chrome shipments to Germany. Moscow said the envoy to Spain, which is reducing wolfram shipments, had been summoned while the Minister to Stockholm, where the Allies are seeking reductions of bearing exports, also was to be called.

The War In Asia

British Open Counterdrive At Kohima

By the United Press

SOUTHEAST ASIA H. Q., Kandy, Ceylon, May 5—British troops have launched a general counter-offensive on the Kohima front and are making satisfactory progress," while in North Burma Chinese troops, led by American tanks, have captured Inkagahtawng and trapped its Japanese garrison of 1000 men, it was announced tonight.

A communique from Admiral Lord Louis Mountbatten's headquarters revealed that "our troops are attacking at all points" around Kohima, seeking to remove the threat to Eastern India.

The counter-offensive was carefully timed to strike less than two weeks before the monsoon, so that once the Japanese are dislodged from their stubbornly held positions and thrown into retreat, the weather will spur on their disaster.

POWERFUL SUPPORT

A final spell of fair weather enabled British and American planes to contribute powerful supporting attacks against Japanese communications extending to the Mandalay area, where railroad yards and military stores were blasted.

In capturing Inkagahtawng, Lieutenant General Joseph W. Stilwell's Chinese and American units gained a level route to Kaimang, 18 miles to the south across dusty paddy fields that will not be flooded for at least three weeks. Other Chinese units were only 10 miles from Kaimang at Manpin, but were outside the flat valley which provides the best approach to the Japanese stronghold.

Front dispatches said that Inkagahtawng, a strategic position rather than a town since not even one hut is situated there, fell to an American tank attack after planes had almost obliterated the enemy defenses. American P-51 Mustangs and P-40 Warhawks dumped more than 15 tons of bombs on an area 1500 yards square.

A ROAD BLOCK

Meanwhile, a Chinese flying column slipped around the Japanese positions and threw a road block across the enemy's only trail of escape at a point two miles south of Inkagahtawng. A battalion of about 1000 Japanese was trapped. Allied casualties in the entire operations were only a few men killed or wounded.

Mountbatten's communique reported only minor clashes in the Imphal area south of Kohima, where a few days ago the Japanese appeared about to launch a major attack. Allied patrols found hundreds of bodies of Japanese killed in the recent heavy fighting in that sector.

Aimee McPherson Seriously Ill

LOS ANGELES, May 5 (UP)—Evangelist Aime Semple McPherson was seriously ill at her hilltop home today, her son, Rolf McPherson, reported.

Mrs. McPherson is suffering from an infection which followed a tropical fever she contracted in Mexico and has been ill intermittently for more than a year.

21st Day of Raids

Allied Bombers Blast Huge Dam in Italy, Nazi Strongholds Periled

German Defenses Near the Adriatic Are Threatened; U. S. Heavies Hit Rail Yards at Ploesti

By the Associated Press

LONDON, May 5—American and British dive bombers of the Mediterranean command in a notable coup cracked open the huge Pescara dam in Italy this afternoon, releasing a great wall of flood water which threatened to engulf German strongholds near the Adriatic coast and sweep away bridges vital to Axis military traffic in that long-stalemated sector.

At the same time American heavy bombers striking into Romania hit rail yards at the oil center of Ploesti and at Turnu-Severin near the Danube "iron gate" on the 21st straight day of the two-way pre-invasion sky offensive which is softening up the Atlantic wall and giving direct support to the Red Army in the East.

Italy-based American bomber fleets also struck Podgorica, Yugoslavia, where a big German garrison is located.

Meantime, hundreds of U. S. Liberators and Allied planes from Britain smashed the French Calais anti-invasion defenses and strings of freight cars on rail feeder lines behind it.

ATTACK ON IRAN

Mustang and Kittyhawk fighter-bombers with American pilots in the vanguard made the attack on the Pescara dam near Torre de Passeri, 19 miles up the Pescala river from the port of the same name on the Adriatic side of the Italian peninsula opposite Rome.

The stroke ranked spectacularly with the RAF's successful attack last year on the Mohne dam in Germany.

The Pescara dam's iron sluice gates were ripped apart by underwater explosions from bombs in a 20-minute attack.

As the last Allied flyer left the scene a high wall of water followed by five even higher waves already was a mile downstream, rushing swiftly toward German-occupied Italian cities and Axis defenses erected opposite the British Eighth Army lines in the Orton sector, 10 miles below the port of Pescara.

ANOTHER BREAK

A bomb from the plane of Sergeant Alexander Duguid of Scotland apparently was the first to breach the dam, and Ken Richards, an Australian Kittyhawk pilot, saw his explosives make another break in the iron walls.

American Mustang pilots made the

Continued on Page 3, Col. 3

Extortionist Faints At Long Sentence

NEW YORK, May 5 (UP)—Jacob (Gurrah) Shapiro, erstwhile tough partner of the late Louis (Lepke) Buchalter, fainted in General Sessions Court today after he was sentenced to from 15 years to life for extortion.

With tears streaming down his face, Shapiro trembled and gulped one sedative pill after another as he heard Judge John A. Mullen pass mandatory sentence on him as a fourth offender.

"Thank you, Judge, thank you," he mumbled. Attendants helped him from the courtroom and he collapsed in the lobby. A physician revived him within a few minutes.

Nazis Pour Into Norway And Denmark

By the Associated Press

LONDON, May 5—The Germans were reported tonight to have sent 20,000 reinforcements into restive Denmark and 30,000 into Norway in a new series of anti-invasion moves ranging along almost the entire Western front.

Berlin radio commentators continued to discuss the expected Allied assault as being imminent.

A high percentage of seasoned veterans was included among the troops rushed to the Danish and Norwegian sectors of Germany's western defenses, said reports received here through Stockholm.

FLANDERS' FLOODS

The Belgian News Agency said the Germans had flooded the coastal sone both east and west of Flanders, inundating most roads. This flooding, the news agency added, although undertaken to check invaders, has forced the Nazis to take special protective measures with their defense works between the sea and the submerged inland regions.

Especially in the neighborhood of Calais, Dunkerque, Gravelines and Nieuport rising water and displaced sands from dunes are threatening the defense construction, it was said.

The Germans announced they were ready for assault from any direction, drawing their latest omen from Iceland with a report that there was "great Allied activity and large shipping concentrations there, reinforcing the impression that the Allies are planning an invasion of Scandinavia."

"GREAT GRAVITY"

The Paris radio saw "great gravity" in the west, and Berlin and Vichy commentators noted "mounting Allied reinforcements" in Italy and predicted a blow there simultaneously with the offensive from the west. Algiers said the Germans were rushing fortifications on the island of Elba, lying between Corsica and the Italian northwest coast.

Black Market Whisky Trial

Union Agent Is Named as 'Go-Between'

Jack Goldberger, a union business agent and former ration board member, was named as a "go between" in the whisky black market yesterday at the trial of Frank DePaolo, liquor concern salesmanager, charged with conspiracy to sell liquor above ceiling prices.

Jack Reynolds, an Alameda county AFL union leader, has pleaded guilty to the same charge.

The name of Goldberger was brought into the case to the surprise of Assistant United States Attorney Al Zirpoli. Goldberger is not under indictment, but Zirpoli said an effort will be made to bring him into court.

Goldberger was dragged into the case in Federal Judge Welch's court by Attorney Harold Faulkner, counsel for DePaolo, in an effort to refute the Government's contention that DePaolo was active in soliciting illegal whisky deals.

William Sylvester, a member of the Newspaper and Periodical Drivers and Helpers' Union, Local 921, of which Goldberger is business agent, testifying as a witness for DePaolo, said that he had introduced Goldberger and DePaolo after Goldberger had asked him if he "knew anyone who would be interested in quite a lot of whisky."

Sylvester said he did this merely "as a favor to a friend," that there was nothing in it for him.

DePaolo later testified the transaction, involving 1500 cases of Baltimore Club Special Reserve bourbon, was subsequently completed, but denied there was a violation of the law.

The Office of Price Administration, in obtaining last year a Federal order restraining the Rolandelli Company from selling this whisky above the $27 ceiling price, claimed the liquor was sold for as much as $50 a case. DePaolo is salesmanager for this company.

DePaolo denied that he had ever known Jack Reynolds, who after pleading guilty, had testified to alleged dealings with DePaolo in illicit handling of liquor. On Thanksgiving Day, when Reynolds declared he had discussed the proposed deal with him, DePaolo asserted he was enjoying the holiday dinner with his family.

Goldberger resigned last February as a member of War Price and Ration Board No. 8.

The Index

Casualties	2
Churches	10
Comics	2H
Crossword	9
Drama	8
Editorials	12
Financial	4H
Lichty Cartoon	11
Radio Log	6
Ration Dates	11
Society	10
Vital Statistics	9
COLUMNS	
Bookman's Notebook	12
Will Connolly	1H
Lyons Den	4
Washington Merry-Go-Round	12
Harry B. Smith	2H
Bill Leiser	1H
Chester Rowell	12

Listen to The Chronicle - KYA Time - Clocked News — 1260 on your dial — 6 a. m. to midnight

Gandhi Will Be Freed Today Because of Failing Health

LONDON, May 5 (AP)—Mohandas K. Gandhi, the Indian leader, will be released from internment tomorrow morning.

A statement issued tonight simultaneously in London and India said: "In view of medical reports of Mr. Gandhi's health, the government of India have decided to release him unconditionally. This decision has been taken solely on medical grounds. The release takes place at 8 a. m. May 6.

The 75-year-old leader in the struggle for Indian freedom has been imprisoned in the ornate palace of the Aga Khan at Poona since August, 1942, because of his attitude toward India's resistance to Japan.

He developed a fever last month less than two months after the death of his wife, and although he showed improvement his general condition caused anxiety.

For 40 years he has been a dominant figure in the life of India, called the Mahatma (Great Soul) during most of his career as a nationalist leader and variously regarded as a saint, a revolutionary and a reactionary, a patriot and an unscrupulous politician. Millions in teeming India regard him as nothing less than a god.

His favorite weapon to rouse the masses have been his fasts and his civil disobedience campaign.

Weather Man

"Was worried about the Army and Ward's," said Anemometer.

"Why wus you worried?" demanded the Weather Man.

"In case the Army'd get out a catalogue."

"That's part of the business."

"But how'd you know what you were buyin'? You'd get items listed like this: G B in hars. Fst stl. Solve rat prob by rsg own vegs. Or BB sted."

"What's wrg with that? It's clr as mud to me," and the W. M. cooked up a couple of isotherms and got tdy's frost: FAIR.

The Cincinnati Post

Late News
Home Edition

VOL. 122 NO. 128 — CINCINNATI, MONDAY, DECEMBER 8, 1941 — PRICE THREE CENTS

CONGRESS VOTES WAR;
WOMAN CASTS LONE 'NO'

HAWAII'S DEAD 1500; NAVAL BATTLE RAGES

Pacific Ocean Becomes Vast

THE WEATHER

The Detroit N

TUESDAY, DECEMBER 9, 1941, 69th Year, No. 199 — THE HOME NEWSPAPER

ENEMY PLANES R
2 HOURS FROM N

Japs Take

THIS IS THE TIME FOR ALL GOOD MEN AND WOMEN TO AID OUR SOLDIERS. BUY WAR BONDS TODAY!

THE DAILY TIMES HERALD

FINAL EDITION

DALLAS, TEXAS — The Only Newspaper in Dallas With the Day ASSOCIATED PRESS News and Day Wirephoto Service

VOL. LXIV No. 353 — DALLAS, TEXAS, THURSDAY EVENING, APRIL 9, 1942. 32 Pages — PRICE

36,852 BATAAN DEFENDERS
FACE DEATH OR SURRENDER

MARSHALL'S REMARK CAUSES RUMORS OF "SECOND FRONT"

Japs Roll Back Bataan Defenders

BATAAN

EXHAUSTION CLOSES SAGA OF BRAVERY

MANY BELIEVE NORWAY BEST PLACE TO HIT

Darwin House Wrecked by Bombs

TWO BRITISH CRUISERS SUNK BY JAPANESE

THE WEATHER

Times He

VOL V, NO. 77 — WASHINGTON, D.C. — SUNDAY

U.S. Freezes 27 Million Wo

16 Forts Lost In Big Attack On Bremen

Blast Focke-Wulf Plant; 50 Nazis Shot Down

Setting the Rising Sun:
U.S. Subs Sink 5 Jap Ships; Kiska Hit 13 Times in Day

Nipponese Air Base Held Serious Menace As Work Progresses Despite 96 Attacks

4,680 Taken Prisoner by Eisenhower

House Kills Incentive Pay For Farmers

3rd WAR LOAN — Buy More Bonds

DAILY WORLD

3rd WAR LOAN — Buy an Extra $100 Bond

Each Star Represents a Former Daily World Employee In The Service — Opelousas, Louisiana,

Volume IV, — Friday, October 1, 1943

NAPLES FALLS TO ALLIES
BOND RALLY A HUGE SUCCESS

Once A Beautiful Now Rubbish

Save Those Tin Can
Country Needs Them

Russian Army Smashing Closer to Fortress Guarding Berlin

FORT WORTH STAR-TELEGRAM

EVENING

LARGEST CIRCULATION IN TEXAS OVER 175,000 DAILY — A Fort Worth Owned Newspaper

SIXTY FIFTH YEAR NO. 17. — FORT WORTH, TEXAS — "Where the West Begins" — SATURDAY FEBRUARY 17, 1945 — EIGHT PAGES — PRICE FIVE CENTS

IWO JIMA AND CORREGIDOR
INVADED, JAPANESE REPORT

Reds Closer To Fortress Near Berlin

Tokio Claims Five

Buff

VOL. CXX—NO. 99

Atomic B
Equals 2

SENATE WILL VOTE ON UNLIMITED USE OF PEACE TROOPS

DEPARTMENTAL INDEX

The Times-Picayune

YEAR—NO. 104 — NEW ORLEANS, TUESDAY, MAY 8, 1945 — SINGLE COPY 5 CENTS

THE SCENE SHIFTS

V-E PROCLAMATIONS AWAITED TODAY

BIG 3 WILL GIVE

The Industrial Muscle

Late in 1943, at a meeting between F.D.R., Churchill and Stalin in Teheran, the Russian leader offered a toast: "To American production, without which this war would have been lost." As Stalin spoke, Russian soldiers in U.S. trucks and jeeps were rolling the Nazis back on the 2,000-mile front. Just as toastworthy was the speed with which America had turned to the making of munitions. In 1939 only 2 per cent of the gross national output was armaments. But in the year after Pearl Harbor war production quadrupled; and by 1944 American assembly lines were spewing out 50 per cent more armaments than the Axis nations. Not all of the American production was first class: hastily welded Liberty Ships were known to break apart in heavy seas; the Sherman tank was considered more vulnerable than the German Tiger tank; and American torpedoes were notorious for malfunctioning (one frustrated U.S. submarine crew, with Japan's largest oil tanker sitting unprotected in its sights, hit the ship with eight duds before running out of ammunition). Nevertheless, most U.S. weapons were at least the equal of their Axis counterparts. And the continuing volume of production was so great that the enemy was eventually crushed beneath a weight of weaponry.

Sour Grapes from Germany

A vital part of America's wartime strength was girlpower. In the five months after Pearl Harbor 750,000 women volunteered for duty at armament plants. At first, managers in heavy industry were leery of using women workers —only 80,000 of the early volunteers won prompt assignments. But by 1944, some 3.5 million women stood side by side with 6 million men on the assembly lines, turning out entire cargo ships in 17 days, reducing the time needed to make a bomber from 200,000 man-hours to 13,000. In the process they helped win the coveted Army-Navy "E" pennant for excellence in meeting awesome weapons quotas—and also earned a sour bleat *(below)* from Hitler's propaganda minister, who refused to acknowledge the overwhelming triumphs of U.S. war production.

The Americans are so helpless that they must fall back again and again upon boasting about their matériel. Their loud mouths produce a thousand airplanes and tanks almost daily, but when they need them they haven't got them and are therefore taking one beating after another. JOSEPH GOEBBELS

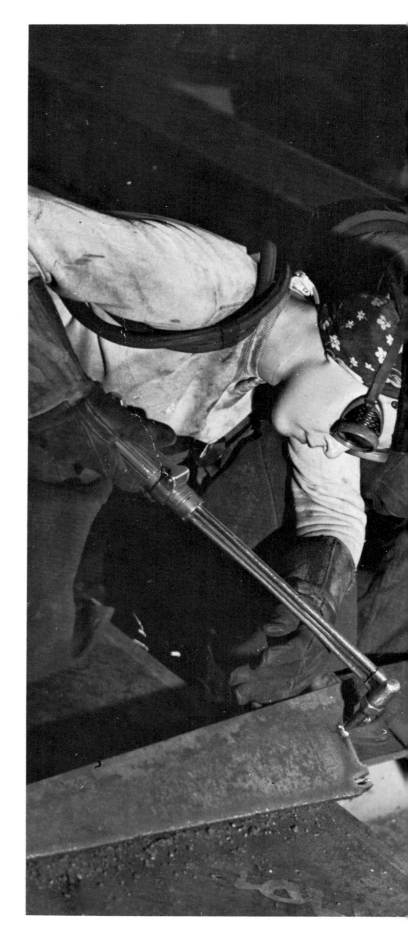

Women workers bevel armor plating with acetylene torches. "For all of them, slacks have become the badge of honor," wrote columnist Max Lerner.

Workmen at Calship Yards, Los Angeles, take a short break from building Victory cargo ships; 247 were launched in the first 212 days of 1945.

In the month that Stalin saluted U.S. production—and a full half year before the invasion of Normandy—America had built such an enormous storehouse of armaments that Washington ordered some defense plants to stop hiring and to cut back on items like anti-tank guns and trainer planes. And throughout 1944 government committees were already drawing up plans to reconvert the war machine to peacetime production. By the end of the war American factories had run up the five-year totals at right. Yet so vast was the nation's overall productive muscle that all during the war America always made more butter than guns: in no single year did armaments account for more than 40 per cent of the gross national product.

War Production	
July 1, 1940 to July 31, 1945	
AIRCRAFT	296,429
NAVAL SHIPS	71,062
CARGO SHIPS	5,425
ARTILLERY	372,431
SMALL ARMS	20,086,061
SMALL ARMS AMMUNITION (rounds)	41,585,000,000
AIRCRAFT BOMBS (tons)	5,822,000
TANKS AND SELF-PROPELLED GUNS	102,351
TRUCKS	2,455,964

Inspectors check over a tank before it rumbles out of the Chrysler Arsenal. The country's largest tank factory, Chrysler produced a total of 25,507.

Over 6,000 Corsairs—fighter planes with fold-up wings for use on board aircraft carriers—rolled out of this plant in Stratford, Connecticut.

A Common Cause

No other event in the 20th Century matched Pearl Harbor in uniting the U.S. On December 8, 1941, the vote in Congress was 470 to 1 to declare war; the one dissenter, pacifist Jeanette Rankin, simply did not believe Hawaii had been bombed. Across the nation, everyone knew what the fighting was about. "Hitler" became a synonym for mindless tyranny ("You're a Hitler, Joe Smith; I don't know why I ever married you"); and "Jap" became, among teenagers, a verb meaning to betray ("I introduced this guy to my girl, and he Japped me"). Yet many people felt frustrated. The shooting was far away and there were only so many war-production jobs to go around. As a result, trying to be part of the action, U.S. citizens bought $49 billion in War Bonds. They grew their own food in Victory Gardens —even though American farmers were producing enough to feed half a world and its armies. Thousands of miles from real bombing, volunteers formed an enormous Civilian Defense corps. While the world's greatest industrial complex was fueled by a vast reservoir of natural resources, children saved their empty toothpaste tubes for scrap-metal drives. These efforts made all Americans feel they were in the game—and actually did help to shorten the conflict *(pages 162-163)*.

SAVE FREEDOM OF SPEECH

BUY WAR BONDS

1944

WAR FUND

Moisten gummed edges
and apply to
window

AMERICA CALLING

Take your place in
Civilian Defense

☆ ☆ ☆ ☆ ☆ ☆ ☆ ☆ ☆ ☆ ☆ ☆ ☆ ☆ ☆ ☆

Sky Pilots

Although not one ground-based airplane of the Axis powers was within combat range of the U.S., every American town was cluttered with earnest Civilian Defense volunteers. Air raid wardens ran around enforcing unnecessary blackouts while spotters scanned the friendly skies for hostile craft. Of course, not one of the 1.5 million spotters ever saw an enemy plane, and over-eager air raid wardens sometimes exasperated professionals like the New York police captain quoted below. But the volunteers kept trying, and often performed genuine community services.

During the hurricane, 25,000 wardens turned out to help the police. They did some wonderful heroic things that just weren't sensible like running around picking up live wires and fixing gas leaks. It was just by the grace of God that none of them were hurt. Some wardens are too enthusiastic. During the last blackout, a switch got stuck at Coney Island, and the wardens tried to fix it themselves instead of calling for help right away. It sure was nice of them to try, but it wasted a lot of valuable time.

An air spotter struggles to memorize the silhouettes of enemy planes as he stands a cold watch at a Civilian Defense post in Kent, Connecticut.

Vitamins for Victory

At the end of December 1941 Secretary of Agriculture Claude R. Wickard startled Americans by suggesting that because commercial farmers were busy feeding the Army, U.S. civilians who wanted fresh vegetables on their tables should plant Victory Gardens. With that, millions of home-front citizens who had never known a hoe from a trowel began planting lettuce, tomatoes, beets, carrots, peas and radishes in such unlikely sites as their own backyards, the Portland (Oregon) Zoo, Chicago's Arlington Racetrack and the yard of the Cook County Jail.

To help the amateurs, the Department of Agriculture and seed companies, in reams of material, told when to plant what, warned against tenderheartedness when it came to thinning one's own precious seedlings and illustrated the spoilage signs of melon anthracnose and onion smudge. The results were astounding. The garden at right in eight months yielded 30 pounds of tomatoes, 100 ears of corn, 150 radishes, 35 heads of lettuce and 75 heads of hearty cabbage. In Tennessee Sunday farmers who grew 75 per cent of their food received the State Certificate of Recognition (above). In 1943 alone, Sunday farmers planted 20.5 million plots and produced at least one third of all the fresh vegetables consumed in the country.

At his parking lot in downtown New Orleans, a block from the heavy traffic of Canal Street, Victory Gardener Harry Ducote tends his cabbages.

Identical twins Mary and Marjorie Vaughan of West Lafayette, Indiana, roll two of 2.5 billion bandages Red Cross wartime volunteers made.

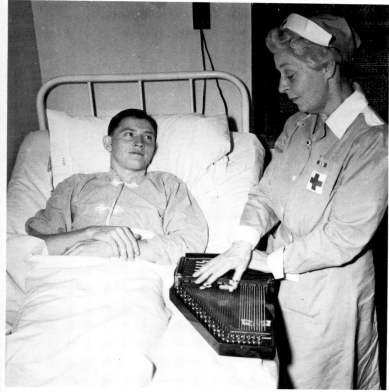

Twanging her autoharp, a Red Cross Gray Lady soothes a wounded soldier.

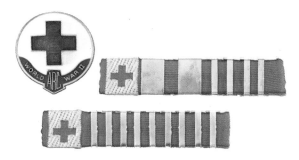

Red Cross volunteers give magazines to U.S. servicemen on a troop train.

The Greatest Mother

When war suddenly fell upon the U.S., the only American organization that seemed ready to act was the Red Cross. Small wonder. The Red Cross had had 59 years of practice conducting disaster and relief programs; and with its experience in World War I—when it first called itself "The Greatest Mother" during a fund-raising drive—it was keyed to rush trained civilian aid to modern armed forces.

The day after Pearl Harbor 3,740 Red Cross chapters rallied tens of thousands of volunteers to roll bandages, amuse the wounded and carry out other merciful tasks that might help win the war. Throughout the conflict the enormous Red Cross emergency blood bank program collected 13.3 million units of blood for plasma from 6.66 million queasy volunteer donors.

The only reward Red Cross volunteers received for their millions of hours of work was the private satisfaction of doing a needed job—plus cherished Red Cross pins and service ribbons. Proudly worn over the uniform pocket, the ribbons *(above)* had stripes of silver for every 500 hours of service, thin gold stripes for 1,000 hours and wide gold stripes for 5,000 hours. The upper ribbon, worn by a small elite corps, represents a staggering 14,000 hours of Red Cross work—or 10 hours for every day of the war.

A citizen volunteer gathers up bushel baskets of flattened tin cans.

A patriot turns in her stockings to make powder bags for naval guns.

An official in Detroit examines a pile of bronze and steel padlocks.

A housewife turns in some bacon grease, used in making ammunition.

A junk dealer exhibits waste paper that will make packing cartons.

A rubber drive in Raleigh, North Carolina, produces a heap of worn tires.

JUNK MAKES FIGHTING WEAPONS

One old radiator will provide scrap steel needed for seventeen .30 calibre rifles.

One old lawn mower will help make six 3-inch shells.

One useless old tire will provide as much rubber as is used in 12 gas masks.

One old shovel will help make 4 hand grenades.

Soldiers' wives in Newark, New Jersey, sort out empty toothpaste tubes.

A Happy Mess

To supplement the raw materials needed for defense, America went on the biggest scavenger hunt in its history. Patriotic civilians across the nation began ransacking their attics for discarded overshoes, rusty baby carriages, aluminum pots, tin cans and anything else that could be turned into armaments. In Boston in 1942, the local Brahmins organized a black-tie scrap party that took in, among other items, a horse-drawn buggy, a Civil War Gatling gun and Governor Leverett Saltonstall's rowing machine. The same year, contributions to a nationwide rubber drive included six tons of rubber heels from a Seattle shoemaker, 5,000 tons of car tires from Los Angeles and the rubber mat that supported the favorite spittoon of Senator "Cotton Ed" Smith of South Carolina.

So zealous were the nation's scrap scavengers that the government at first could not handle the load, and piles of debris sometimes accumulated for months before they could be put to use. The Boy Scouts had salvaged so much waste paper (150,000 tons) by June 1942 that the country's paper mills were glutted and the drive was temporarily called off. But the mess of scrap eventually got cleaned up, and by 1945 it was supplying much of the steel, half the tin and half the paper that was needed to win the war.

Going by the Book

For a people almost totally unused to any kind of war-time sacrifice, WPB Directive No. 1 to OPA, January 1942 —instituting rationing—came as a shock. Suddenly, U.S. citizens were stuck with a mess of little books and stamps that limited the food or gas they could buy. What's more, the instructions on how to use the food stamps seemed in-comprehensible *(below)*.

Gasoline rationing was especially unpopular. When the average driver received an "A" card limiting him to a mere three gallons of gas a week, he started to cheat. By late 1942 gas-chiseling became a national scandal but even-tually most drivers turned in the extra cards they had wheedled and made do with the patriotic three gallons.

All RED and BLUE stamps in War Ration Book 4 are WORTH 10 POINTS EACH. RED and BLUE TOKENS are WORTH 1 POINT EACH. RED and BLUE TOKENS are used to make CHANGE for RED and BLUE stamps only when purchase is made. IMPORTANT! POINT VALUES of BROWN and GREEN STAMPS are NOT changed.

At seven in the morning of July 21, 1942, the day before strict gas rationing started, cars jam a Washington, D.C., gas station to fill up.

Cuts of meat, prominently marked with OPA ceiling prices and ration point values, lie displayed on the counter of a butcher shop in March 1943.

Wartime Shopping Guide

Item	Weight	Point Value
PORTERHOUSE STEAK	1 lb.	12
HAMBURGER	1 lb.	7
LOIN LAMB CHOPS	1 lb.	9
HAM	1 lb.	7
BUTTER	1 lb.	16
MARGARINE	1 lb.	4
CANNED SARDINES	1 lb.	12
CANNED MILK	1 lb.	1
AMERICAN CHEDDAR CHEESE	1 lb.	8
DRIED BEEF SLICES	1 lb.	16
PEACHES	16 oz. can	18
CARROTS	16 oz. can	6
PINEAPPLE JUICE	46 oz. can	22
BABY FOODS	4½ oz. jar	1
FROZEN FRUIT JUICES	6 oz. can	1
TOMATO CATSUP	14 oz. bottle	15

Almost everything that Americans really liked to eat —meat, coffee, butter, cheese, sugar—was strictly rationed by a point system that drove housewives and grocers crazy. Officials had devised what they thought would be a highly workable operation: the OPA issued ration books of stamps with point values and assigned specific point values to foods. Housewives paid the grocer stamps as well as cash. The grocer, to replenish his stocks, sent the stamps to his wholesaler. The wholesaler turned the stamps in at his local bank and got credit to buy more food. In practice, the system turned into a heroic snafu. Grocers had to cope with some 14 billion points a month, actually handling about 3.5 billion tiny stamps. Sometimes they ran out of the gummed sheets the government provided to stick the stamps on—causing one wholesaler to haul loose stamps to the bank in bushel baskets. Yet the wartime U.S. was fed better than ever before: in 1945, the last year of the conflict, the Department of Agriculture reported that Americans ate more food and spent more dollars on victuals than at any other time in history.

A baffled grocer puzzles over his government rationing list as he makes a valiant attempt to label his stock with the correct price in points.

The Call to Arms

Immediately after Pearl Harbor the War Department launched the greatest recruiting drive in the nation's history, and by V-J Day it had put nearly 16 million people into uniform. This thorough sweeping-up of manpower had a noticeable effect on America's way of life: men in civvies became scarce on U.S. streets and on college campuses. By the end of the fall term of 1942 three quarters of the undergraduates at Yale had enlisted; and the university had already graduated the class of 1943—six months ahead of time—in order to hustle college-deferred boys into the service faster. Most of these potential recruits searched zealously for an alternative to becoming infantrymen. They were not unpatriotic, just sure there must be more productive ways to spend the war than sitting around in a muddy foxhole with a rifle. Some enrolled in Army or Navy line-officers' training schools; others signed up claiming special vocations—like auto repairman, Russian translator or even lifeguard. A few went to extreme lengths to get into their chosen branch of the service: one high-school student in suburban Philadelphia, his heart set on being an Army fighter pilot, ate so many carrots (good for the eyes, according to contemporary belief) that his skin turned briefly but brightly orange.

"Greeting"

During the war, most males between 18 and 36 discovered in their morning mail a fateful notice *(below)* that began with the word above. Whereupon, they became GIs much like cartoonist George Baker's Sad Sack, who appears below and on the following pages. The break with civilian life was swift and shocking. At one induction center a sergeant, trying to quiet draftees so he could swear them in, repeatedly begged, "Gentlemen, please be quiet." The oath-taking over, he roared, "Now, goddam it, SHUT UP."

SAD SACK

Having submitted yourself to a local board composed of your neighbors for the purpose of determining your availability for training and service in the land or naval forces of the United States, you are hereby notified that you have now been selected for training and service therein. This local board will furnish transportation to an induction station. You will there be examined, and, if accepted . . ., you will then be inducted into the land or naval forces. If you are employed, you should advise your employer of this notice. . . . Your employer can then be prepared to replace you if you are accepted, or to continue your employment if you are rejected. Willful failure to report promptly to this local board at the hour and on the day named . . . is a violation of the Selective Training and Service Act of 1940, as amended, and subjects the violator to fine and imprisonment.

New recruits in civvies march with their overnight bags to the train station in Macon, Georgia, en route to a Navy training school in Norfolk.

"If you've got eyes, ears, and a throat, you're in," said a barracks wit.

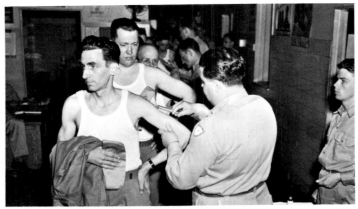

A recruit looks away while he gets the dreaded immunization needle.

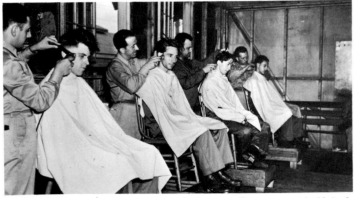

Barbers reduce luxuriant civilian hair to a Spartan one-half inch.

One supply sergeant told gripers, "This ain't Hart, Shaffner, or Marx."

THE SAD SACK   THE UNIFORM

SGT. GEORGE BAKER

From the very beginning of the war, the American GI was the best-equipped soldier in the world. His gear was further improved in 1942 when the chamber-pot helmet and Garand M-1 replaced the old tin hat and Springfield rifle.

LOCKER
  CAP, GARRISON
  CAP, FIELD, COTTON
  JACKET, FIELD
  SHIRT, FLANNEL
  BLOUSE, WOOL
  NECKTIE, KHAKI
  FATIGUES, BLOUSE
  AND TROUSERS
  TROUSERS, WOOL
  UNIFORMS, SUMMER, COTTON

BED (Field Equipment)
  RAINCOAT
  TENT WITH PEGS,
  POLE, ROPE
  UNDERSHIRT, DRAWERS,
  HANDKERCHIEF
  FIRST-AID POUCH
  AND PACKET
  CANTEEN COVER
  CARTRIDGE BELT
  PACK CARRIER
  HAVERSACK, OPEN
  MESS KIT
  TOILET KIT
  SOCKS
  TOWEL
  HELMET, STEEL
  ENTRENCHING TOOL
  BAYONET
  CUP
  CANTEEN
  RIFLE, SPRINGFIELD
  BLANKET, FIELD

FOOTLOCKER
  SOCKS, WOOL AND COTTON
  EXTRA TOILET ARTICLES
  UNDERWEAR,
  TOWELS,
  HANDKERCHIEFS
  SHOES, SERVICE

Beneath the stern eye of a noncom, rookies learn the art of crawling.

Dear *"Mother" of a soldier:*

You may be the mother, wife, aunt, or sister of the soldier I am writing about, or this letter may reach you as the father, uncle, or brother. But as far as he and I are concerned, you are the one at home who thinks of him most often and wonders most frequently what he is doing at Camp Lee.

He will send you many letters telling you, better than I could do, the story of his activities and impressions. My intention is to talk over with you, as one "parent" to another, what it means to send your boy to an Army camp.

Your boy has been assigned for training at Camp Lee's Quartermaster Replacement Training Center. Half his time will be spent in basic military training—learning how to protect himself. He will be taught how to handle weapons, to march erectly and with precision. For the other half of his time here, he will study to become a technician in the Quartermaster Corps.

But the Army isn't all drilling and studying. We know that a soldier must be physically and mentally healthy. Thus our training center has a full athletic program and your boy can compete in almost any sport which happens to be his favorite. Our theatres have the latest movies, and plays by both soldiers and civilians are often presented. And in answer to his religious needs, Camp Lee has many chapels and our chaplains are carefully selected from all principal denominations.

Some reasonable restrictions will be placed on his movements. Except for emergencies, he will not be granted a furlough. He must get up and go to bed at regular and early hours.

I hope that you will put faith in us, as we have put faith in you and your boy. By this, you will be doing your part—just as we are doing ours—to end the threat to democracy everywhere.

Guy I. Rowe, Brigadier General, Q.M.C.

With a practiced drill-manual lunge, a lieutenant guts the "enemy."

Blindfolded and timed, GIs strip and reassemble an M-1 and a carbine.

Under a summer sky, soldiers overhand it through an obstacle course.

A Good Wac Never Gets Pwop

To free able-bodied servicemen for active duty, in May 1942 Secretary of War Stimson authorized a publisher from Texas, Oveta Culp Hobby, to form a Women's Army Auxiliary Corps, later known as the WAC. Male reporters at Mrs. Hobby's first press conference bombarded her with irreverent questions. "Can officer Wacs date privates?" the newsmen asked. "Will Wac's underwear be khaki? What if an unmarried Wac gets pregnant?" Next day and for months to come the papers carried stories about a petticoat army, Wackies and powder magazines.

The press had just as good a time with the Navy's WAVES, the Coast Guard's SPARS and the Women Marines; and the embattled servicewomen got no support from their military brothers. One soldier, writing his sister in order to persuade her not to enlist, asked, "Why can't these gals just stay home and be their own sweet little self, instead of being patriotic?"

In spite of all the boos and catcalls, the women in uniform performed efficiently in posts from Boston to Bataan and contrary to the newsmen's mock concern, almost never got pwop (pregnant without permission). Replacing badly needed manpower, the ladies worked as airplane mechanics, cooks, code clerks, typists and truck drivers. Female pilots ferried planes to Europe. In all, more than 300,000 girls served, most of them with a devoted fervor that often exceeded the men's and occasionally rose to the kind of grown-up Girl-Scout crescendo quoted below.

I *wish I could think of some way I could tell the gals back home what being in the service would do for them. Inside you can say I am doing something. I am helping. I shall continue doing all I can and be grateful for the chance. . . .*

I'm really proud to be here, the places I've been, the great people I've met. That certain feeling I get when I stand at retreat, the chill that the "Star Spangled Banner" sends down my back.

Trim, necktied Wacs stoically sweat through their first gas mask drill.

A hard-boiled Woman Marine jujitsu teacher (left) blocks a knee-kick.

An appreciative visiting officer checks Wacs for straight stocking seams.

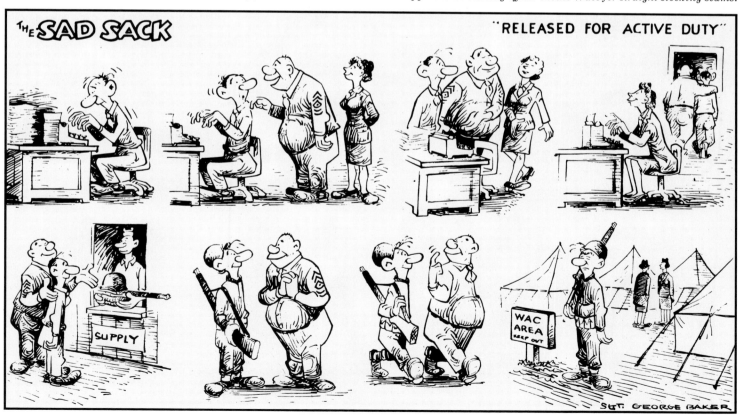

THE SAD SACK

"RELEASED FOR ACTIVE DUTY"

SGT. GEORGE BAKER

Big Night with the Broads

All through boot camp and subsequent tours of duty, every serviceman lived for the days when he would go on leave or liberty. Burning in his mind were wild tales, told by veterans, of booze and broads and orgies. But when the eager GI or swab-jockey finally set off, clutching a pass on which he had signed the stern warning *(right)* on the back, he was usually in for a sharp letdown. Most towns near big service bases, like Leesville, outside Fort Polk, Louisiana, were tiny or dull or both. Boastful Don Juans filled every barracks, but the majority of leaves were like those shown in the scenes below and at right.

While on pass you will be observed by civilians who will judge the United States Army by your appearance and conduct as an individual. Failure on your part to conform to regulations with respect to wearing your uniform and to live up to the highest traditions of the service will result in unfavorable criticism of your Army, your organization, and yourself. I have read and understand the above statement and am familiar with the provisions of paragraphs 1 to 59 of the Soldier's Handbook.

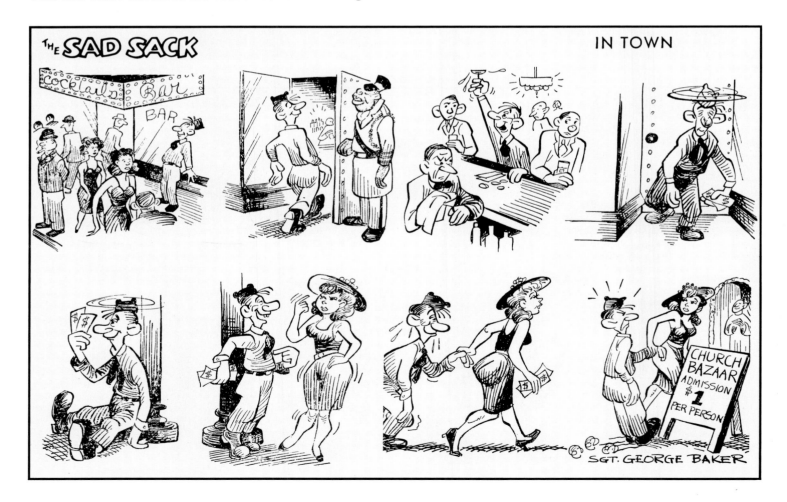

Too broke to dredge up any action—or even so much as a room—in Spokane, Washington, five exhausted fighting men flake out in the local U S O.

War Comes to Fantasyland

Song writers, cartoonists, movie makers and virtually all the other creative people who in peacetime kept America entertained with happy fantasies pitched in to help, somehow, with the war effort. *The Saturday Evening Post's* top illustrator, Norman Rockwell, provided the home front with its favorite make-believe soldier, Willie Gillis; in another burst of popular genius, he drew Rosie, the Riveter, a character who gently satirized the millions of patriotic women who went into war work. For the *Post* cover of Rosie at right, Rockwell borrowed a dignified pose from one created by Michelangelo for the Sistine Chapel frescoes. Designed originally for the prophet Isaiah and embellished by Rockwell with coveralls, rivet gun, ham sandwich, etc., the posture suited Rosie admirably.

Paradoxically, the most formidable fantasy hero of all, Superman, remained a noncombatant. Supersurprisingly, the man of steel was ruled 4-F by his draft board. His X-ray vision betrayed him: when he took his pre-induction physical early in the war, he was given an eye test; without realizing it he looked right through the eye chart and the wall—and read the letters on another chart in the next room. Rejected, he spent the war pushing the Red Cross and V-Bonds.

In 1940 cartoonist Ham Fisher's mythical boxer, Joe Palooka, joined the Army, boosting the draft so effectively that F.D.R. personally thanked Fisher.

The Funnies Fight the Fascists...

When American men went to war, so did American funny-paper characters.
Smilin' Jack joined the Army Air Force. Terry fought Japs instead
of Pirates. And while Daddy Warbucks served as a general, his adopted waif,
Little Orphan Annie, exhorted real kids to collect scrap metal.

...and Hollywood Pitches In

*By January 1942 film makers were hard at work on their
own versions of the struggle overseas. The heroes, naturally, were gallant
American servicemen, the villains a foul brew of sadistic Germans,
bumbling Italians always on the retreat and wily, buck-toothed Japanese.*

The Purple Heart

"Singapore . . . Hong Kong . . . the Indies . . . Thailand!"
gloats a slant-eyed Japanese general, played by Richard Loo,
as he ticks off yellow conquests for captured bomber pilot Dana
Andrews. He and his American melting-pot crew (Ross, Canelli,
Clinton, Skvoznik, Vincent, Greenbaum, Bayforth and Stoner)
are on trial for war crimes. Offered mercy if they reveal the site
of their base, the Americans choose courtroom silence, broken
only by Andrews' defiant speech: "This is your war. . . . You
wanted it. . . . You started it! And now you're going to get it,
and it won't be finished until your dirty little empire is wiped
off the face of the earth!" Whereupon the mortified Loo commits
hara-kiri as the stoic U.S. airmen are sentenced to death.

Above Suspicion

Honeymooners Fred MacMurray and Joan Crawford are asked by the British to sneak Nazi plans for world conquest out of pre-war Germany. Despite much bungling, they outfumble the pursuing Gestapo (above), partly on the strength of such foxy dialogue as: Nazi (saluting), "Heil Hitler!" MacMurray, "Nuts to you, dope!" Nazi (puzzled), "Was heisst das 'dope'?"

Keep Your Powder Dry

In a comedy aimed at promoting the Woman's Army Corps, a socialite (Lana Turner, right) joins the WACs to prove herself worthy of her huge inheritance. At first the cheekiest recruit on the base—above she asks "Had your distributor points cleaned lately, General?"—Lana soon finds WAC life rewarding and by film's end she has tearfully accepted an officer's commission.

Five Graves to Cairo

For most of this reenactment of Nazi General Erwin Rommel's African campaign, Erich von Stroheim (right) portrays the German as a shrewd, cocky—and not unlikable—leader. But to satisfy Hollywood's image of the hateable Hun, he turns sadistic in the last reel, then causes his own defeat at El Alamein by arrogantly bragging of his plans to an Allied double agent.

Air Force

This epic records the adventures of a mythical B-17, the "Mary Ann." The film's remarkable authenticity is ruined at the end when John Garfield (above), as Gunner Winocki, is so enraged at a Jap Zero for strafing a parachuting American that he grabs a .50-caliber machine gun and hip-shoots the Zero down: in fact the gun's recoil would have knocked Garfield flatter than the Zero.

THE SATURDAY EVENING
POST
SEPTEMBER 16, 1944   10¢

Great Great Great Grandpa Gillis

Great Great Grandpa Gillis

Great Grandpa Gillis

Grandpa Gillis

"Fighting Bill" Gillis

Gillis

your son
Willie Gillis

norman
rockwell

THEY SPARKED THE
CARRIER REVOLUTION
BY JACK ALEXANDER
—
HOW SHALL WE RECONVERT
TO PEACETIME WORK?
MAURY MAVERICK
LOUIS RUTHENBURG

Everyboy

*To millions of American mothers, Willie Gillis, the jug-eared GI created
by Norman Rockwell for a series of 11 "Saturday Evening Post" covers, personified their
own sons gone to war. There really was a Willie Gillis; his name was Bob Buck,
and he was a Vermont neighbor of Rockwell's who posed as the model for Gillis, went off
to war, and—like Willy (below right)—finally returned home safe to Mom.*

Bugle Calls from Tin Pan Alley

Early in 1942 Frank Loesser read about the embattled
chaplain at Pearl Harbor who had told his flock to "praise the Lord
and pass the ammunition." The heroic words gave Loesser
the title line for a hit song, one of a flood of popular war ballads.

Light Look at a Dark Time

*While Hollywood cranked out straight-faced clinkers about
the war and funny-paper artists solemnly sent their own heroes off to fight, magazine
cartoonists—especially in "Esquire" and "The New Yorker"—poked
unabashed fun at the home-front chaos of shortages, spy scares and rationing.*

"I had quite a time persuading the Smithsonian to give it back to me, as you may imagine."

"Hello, shipyard? Madam will be a bit
late punching the time clock this morning—she had
the Vanderbilts to dinner last night."
© 1943 BY ESQUIRE, INC.

"Goodbye, darling. Come home early. Remember, I
promised you for the air-raid drill tonight. You're to be a
victim pinned under a pole in front of the A.&P."

"It might be well to encourage some
talking, don't you think?"
© 1944 BY ESQUIRE, INC.

"I'm just frying the white of the egg for you, dear,
tomorrow you can have the yolk."
© 1943 BY ESQUIRE, INC.

"They're related by Red Cross blood."
© 1944 BY ESQUIRE, INC.

"We saved thirteen points sending Junior to bed without his supper."
© 1944 BY ESQUIRE, INC.

"We never thought we'd have to use these antiques
when we bought them."
© 1943 BY ESQUIRE, INC.

"So this GI goes AWOL for a coupla hours to put a fin on a gee-gee
in the sixth and the CO busts him down to a buck
—the filly comes in 20-to-1 and now the old man is trying to G-2
him for hot tips with three up and two down for bait."
© 1943 BY ESQUIRE, INC.

"He says it's not that he wants the beer so much, but they need the bottle caps for the war effort!"

The Enemy Within

As war clouds gathered on America's horizons, the country began to worry about spies. The biggest nonfiction best seller of 1943, John Roy Carlson's witch-chaser, *Undercover,* claimed 200 fascist organizations in the U.S. were spreading the Hitler line that the war was a Jewish-British plot; and it detailed the alleged fascist ties of Charles Lindbergh and Father Charles Coughlin. The book brought on a rash of "revelations"—such as that 407 New York police were secret members of a militant right-wing Christian Front organization (they were) and that most of the Japanese in Hawaii were enemy agents (they weren't).

The government contributed its share to the nation's unease. Propagandists ordered up posters like those at right, and at Cabinet meetings Roosevelt scowled at Attorney General Francis Biddle, asking him when he was going to do something. But Biddle was a fastidious civil libertarian, and he rejected F.D.R.'s impetuous request that he intern all 600,000 German aliens. During most of the war, Biddle managed to keep down the lynch-party impulses of homefront commandos. One piece of mass vigilantism slipped past over his protests: the shameful internment of 125,000 Japanese-Americans *(pages 200-207).*

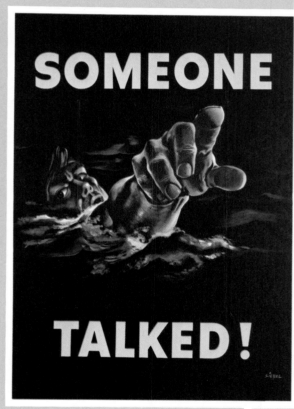

SOMEONE

TALKED!

AWARD

FOR CARELESS TALK

DON'T DISCUSS TROOP MOVEMENTS · SHIP SAILINGS · WAR EQUIPMENT

...because somebody talked!

A U.S. tanker burns from a torpedo hit off Florida, in 1943. A tanker was a favorite target for Nazi subs: it sank easily and its cargo was vital.

A Flicker of the War

While its allies in Europe were reeling under enemy occupation and air raids, the U.S. at home experienced only occasional flickers of war. Most grim and threatening was the massacre of allied ships in 1942 and 1943 by Nazi subs lying right off the East Coast. The U-boats made easy targets of freighters and tankers outlined against the glare of cities like Miami, whose six miles of neon glow shone far out to sea; almost nightly, terrified, oil-begrimed survivors staggered ashore onto beaches from Florida to New Jersey. At the height of the U-boat activity, many Americans were convinced that ship locations were being disclosed by spies. But although G-men arrested some 4,000 espionage suspects from 1938 to the end of the war, not a single ship-sinking was traced to signals from shore. In all, only 94 of the FBI's suspects were ever convicted, and few of these accomplished much before they were caught. After investigating 19,649 reported cases of sabotage, the FBI found that not one was enemy-directed.

An FBI raid on German aliens in Detroit, carried out right after Pearl Harbor, turns up a small arsenal of handguns, rifles and shotguns.

The Submarine Caper

In the dark hours of June 13, 1942, a rubber boat slipped out of the fog onto the beach at Amagansett, Long Island, and discharged four men and four stout crates. Four nights later, on a beach in Florida, another sub discharged four more men with similar boxes.

Adolf Hitler was preparing to open battle on American soil. The eight boxes held enough explosives to carry on a two-year program for sabotaging U.S. industry and the eight Germans had been hand-picked for the job. Before the war, all had lived in the U.S.; all spoke English fluently; all had enthusiastically quit the U.S. for Nazi Germany; all trained at the *Abwehr*'s dirty-tricks school. The project looked highly serious and expert.

The reality turned out to be more like low comedy—but with a grim denouement. The Long Island sub landed its saboteurs not at Easthampton, as planned, but three miles eastward, just half a mile from a Coast Guard Station. Sure enough, as the four Nazis changed into mufti, up walked a Coast Guardsman and caught them with their pants down and speaking German. George Dasch, the leader, threatened the Guardsman with death, forced on him a $300 bribe and sent him on, assuring the others: "I had him buffaloed." The Guardsman hurried back to report the whole business to his superiors.

Burying their boxes of explosives, the Long Island four headed for a train station. But lacking a compass, they blundered through a trailer camp as lights popped on and voices cried out; they barely managed to get the train. By forenoon that day the Coast Guard had found the boxes and told the FBI that four saboteurs were heading for New York. There, far from sabotaging the U.S. economy, the Nazis were busy supporting it—buying clothes at Rogers Peet, dining at Dinty Moore's, playing high-stakes pinochle and relaxing with B-girls.

By now the other four Nazis were landing in Florida; they split up, two heading for New York and two for Chicago. On his arrival in Chicago, Herbert Haupt told his mother and father his mission and even showed his canvas bag with its false bottom padded with $50 bills. Hermann Neubauer had no family in Chicago. But no mat-

ter; he managed to find someone to blab to. He looked up a German couple whose relative he had met in Germany, and within minutes was telling all.

Once in New York, Edward Kerling of the Florida entourage looked up both his wife and his mistress; Werner Thiel sent word to an old friend to meet him in Grand Central. Meanwhile Heinrich Heinck and Richard Quirin, of the Long Island crew, had found a German-born couple of their own to confide in. Only two men—Dasch and Ernest Burger—did not blab to friends. They blabbed to the FBI. Dasch was plain scared and Burger, an old-time Nazi who had been in a Gestapo jail for 17 months for ideological deviation, was angry.

By June 27, two weeks after they arrived, all eight Germans were in custody and standing trial in a closed military court as enemy soldiers. The Germans were brilliantly defended by Army-appointed counsel; one of them, Colonel Kenneth Royall, appealed to the U.S. Supreme Court for a writ of habeas corpus. In an otherwise sad little tale, this action provided the one touch of magnificence. Solemnly responding to Royall, America's highest court met on July 29, 1942, for its first special session since 1920, to decide, in effect, whether the President had the right to deny eight Nazi saboteurs a civil trial.

After two days the Court denied Royall's motion. The military tribunal had resumed, and on August 3, transmitted 3,000 pages of transcript and its secret verdict to F.D.R., who affirmed it after five days of review. For all but two of the men, the sentence was death. On August 8, 1942, one by one, six saboteurs, their faces masked, were electrocuted in the District of Columbia jail. Dasch and Burger, who had turned themselves in, received jail terms commuted to deportation after the war. Before the other six died, they drafted a statement for Colonel Royall: "We want to state that defense counsel represented our case better than we could expect and probably risked the indignation of public opinion." The Nazis did not quite understand the American sense of justice. Within five years Kenneth Royall had become a member of President Truman's Cabinet and the first Secretary of the Army.

The Long Island Four

GEORGE DASCH

ERNEST BURGER

HEINRICH HEINCK

RICHARD QUIRIN

The Florida Four

EDWARD KERLING

HERBERT HAUPT

HERMANN NEUBAUER

WERNER THIEL

Six of the saboteurs above were executed; Dasch and Burger were imprisoned. In 1944 another Nazi sub landed men; again they were caught.

An eviction notice tacked to their stoop, Japanese-Americans in San Francisco wait for U.S. authorities to herd them off to an internment camp.

No Japs Wanted

When Japan struck Pearl Harbor on December 7, 1941, Americans reacted with a gut impulse for revenge. Understandably, they erupted in rage against the Japanese nation; less creditably, they turned with fury on some of their own neighbors and fellow citizens—the 125,000 men, women and children of Japanese birth or descent who lived in the continental United States. Of that total, 110,000 resided on the West Coast and 70,000 of them had been born on American soil, a fact that made them bona fide American citizens. But in the shock and terror that followed in the wake of Pearl Harbor, white Americans seethed with racism. "A Jap's a Jap!" snapped Lieutenant General John L. De Witt, Commanding General of Western Defense. "It makes no difference whether he is an American or not."

General De Witt had plenty of company. The very day after Pearl Harbor, funds belonging to Japanese-Americans in California were frozen and banks refused to cash their checks. Milkmen refused to deliver their milk; grocers refused to sell them food; insurance companies canceled their policies. A number of cities forbade them to conduct business or even to put out to sea as commercial fishermen. The state of California revoked their licenses to practice either law or medicine and dismissed them from civil service jobs in city, county and state offices from Crescent City to San Diego.

Altogether the Japanese represented only 1 per cent of the population of California and one tenth of 1 per cent of the entire U.S. population—not very threatening figures. Nevertheless, in the months of panic and uncertainty following the destruction of the U.S. Pacific fleet, a resounding chorus echoed all through the Western states, demanding that every Japanese be evacuated from the coastal area at once.

Predictably, the sensational press joined in the hate campaign. "Why treat the Japs well here?" asked a column in a chain of Western newspapers. "They take the parking positions. They get ahead of you in the stamp line at the post office. They have their share of seats on bus and streetcar lines. Let 'em be pinched, hurt, hungry, and dead up against it. . . . Personally I hate the Japanese."

Less predictably, the sober-minded Walter Lippmann added his voice to the chorus. When that venerable dean of American correspondents sounded his forebodings (excerpted, overleaf), the White House itself took notice. Justice Department officials later asserted that the Lippmann column had been among the most important factors in pushing public opinion onto the side of evacuation. Five days after the column appeared, on February 19, President Roosevelt signed Executive Order No. 9066, authorizing the Secretary of War to establish "military areas" and exclude from them "any or all persons." Immediately the order for exclusion was put in force; and with brutal swiftness 110,000 people—the entire Japanese community of the West—were driven out of their homes. In California alone they were deprived of nearly half a billion dollars in yearly income, some $70 million worth of farms and farm equipment, $35 million worth of fruit and vegetable produce, and lifetime savings and assets that no one bothered to calculate. No specific charges were made against these people; no hearings were held to determine whether there was evidence of subversion.

How did it happen? Panic was partly to blame; the Japanese nation was winning the opening engagements of the war, taking Guam, Hong Kong, Manila and Singapore between December and February. It was easy in those frightening months of defeat to believe that the West Coast might be next, and that California, with its tight concentration of Japanese descendants, had 100,000 resident spies. Logic gave way to the feelings of persecution that spring from fear. The Army claimed that the evacuation was a military necessity—heedless of the fact that Japanese in Hawaii had manned machine guns against the attack on Pearl Harbor and worked tirelessly in hospitals to save Caucasian lives. The balance of America went along with California and the Army.

Though war hysteria provided the prime impetus, it was not the only reason for the fate of the Japanese in America. The roots of anti-Japanese sentiment went further back in time than December 7. As far back as the

A bewildered Nisei toddler, tagged like a piece of baggage, stands at the feet of a GI guard while waiting to be taken to an assembly center.

A Nisei girl peers over a pile of evacuees' hand baggage. On arrival at the detention camps, all gear was inspected; liquor and razors were confiscated.

turn of the century, most West Coast farmers and businessmen had welcomed Japanese immigrants for the same reason that other commercially minded Americans welcomed immigrants generally: they provided cheap labor. Until a federal quota of 1924 curtailed Oriental immigration, thousands of young Japanese men poured into the coastal towns and valleys, worked for years to amass some savings, then wrote home for brides and settled down to raise families. Between the arrival of the first Japanese workers, called Issei, and the birth of their children, the Nisei, there was a delay long enough to create a substantial split between the generations.

In 1942, when all hands were interned, most Issei were well along in their middle years or even entering old age; the Nisei were predominantly teenagers or young adults in their twenties. Neither group had much inclination for subversion. The Issei had little or no thought of ever returning to Japan, and the Nisei, most of them public-school kids, were adopting the dress, slang, manners and tastes of their white American contemporaries.

Unlike other immigrants, who quickly dispersed and later mixed with the descendants of earlier settlers, the Japanese concentrated themselves in Little Tokyos that sprang up in the West Coast cities—of necessity, because whites would not assimilate them. In these Oriental enclaves the Issei held to their native language, customs, and even clothing—facts that made them suspiciously alien to the very Americans who refused to take them in. But though they were unabsorbed, the Japanese had, through diligence and frugality, risen to become independent farmers, fishermen, merchants and professional men. By 1940 the farmers among them were producing and distributing from 50 to 90 per cent of the fruit and vegetables that Californians had on their dining tables every day of the year. In standard American tradition, the Japanese had come to labor and had made good.

In equally American fashion, the whites who were one diminishing jump ahead of them watched with apprehension the prospering of the newcomers. "It's a question of whether the white man lives on the Pacific Coast or the brown men," said Austin E. Anson, a member of the Shipper-Grower Association of Salinas, California, lobbying in Washington for evacuation. "They came into this valley to work, and they stayed to take over."

In February 1942, when the authorities decided on evacuation, the Japanese were at first encouraged to leave California voluntarily and to go inland. No fewer than 8,000 Japanese complied in three weeks' time, but that undertaking soon proved fraught with difficulties.

"We feel that if Japs are dangerous in Berkeley, California, they are likewise dangerous to the State of Nevada," declared the Nevada Bar Association. "It is utterly unequitable and unfair to subject Wyoming to the bureaucratic dictum that it shall support and find employment for

Lippmann Looks at the Japanese Menace

It is the fact that the Japanese navy has been reconnoitering the Pacific Coast more or less continually and for a considerable period of time, testing and feeling out the American defenses. It is the fact that communication takes place between the enemy at sea and enemy agents on land. These are facts which we shall ignore or minimize at our peril.

I understand fully and appreciate thoroughly the unwillingness of Washington to adopt a policy of mass evacuation and mass internment of all those who are technically enemy aliens. But I submit that Washington is not defining the problem on the Pacific Coast correctly and that it is failing to deal with the practical issues promptly. The Pacific Coast is officially a combat zone: some part of it may at any moment be a battlefield. Nobody's constitutional rights include the right to reside and do business on a battlefield.

FEBRUARY 12, 1942

Japanese brought here from Pacific Coast defense zones," thundered the *State-Tribune* of Wyoming. "The Japs live like rats, breed like rats and act like rats," said Governor Chase Clark of Idaho. "I don't want them coming into Idaho, and I don't want them taking seats in our university." "Japs are not wanted and not welcome in Kansas," said Governor Payne Ratner, who ordered patrolmen to bar them from the state highways. "Our people are not familiar with the customs or peculiarities of the Japanese," said Arkansas Governor Homer M. Adkins, "and I doubt the wisdom of placing any in Arkansas."

Everywhere the refugees went, gas station attendants refused to fill their tanks; restaurants and barbershops refused to serve them or hung signs in their windows that read: "This restaurant poisons both rats and Japs" or "Japs Shaved: Not Responsible for Accidents."

By March 27 the Japanese who remained in California were told they could no longer evacuate voluntarily but would have to do so under direction of the United States Army. On receiving evacuation orders, the Japanese had 48 hours in which to dispose of their businesses, homes and furnishings before reporting, with whatever belong-

ings they could carry as hand luggage, to 15 Army-run Assembly Centers in or near the cities where they lived. On arrival they were given medical examinations and identification cards and herded into hastily thrown-up barracks. There, like prisoners of war, they were penned in behind barbed wire fences and constantly watched by patrolling Army police. At night searchlights swept the bare ground inside the wire.

Most of the camps were dismal sites indeed. The one in Yakima, Washington, was in a deserted brewery lot; the ones in Santa Anita and Tanforan were race tracks, and the prisoners were lodged in horse stalls. "The stench of manure returned with the heat, and this in turn brought back the horseflies," wrote artist Miné Okubu, some of whose drawings appear below. In Puyallup, Washington, there was one washroom for every 100 families. In other centers the prisoners had to use candles and kerosene lamps for lighting—alongside the flammable straw mattresses on which they bedded down.

In time the War Relocation Authority, created to take over the Japanese internment from the Army, located 10 "suitable" sites inland, and the internees were moved

A Nisei couple clean the horse stall where they have been billeted.

Internees queue up for a meal. Five thousand dined in a single hall.

again. But the new quarters were no more inviting. "This was Topaz!" wrote a Nisei youngster assigned to one in Utah. "We had a hard time to find our home for the barracks were all alike. Topaz looked so big, so enormous to us. It made me feel like an ant. The dust gets in our hair. Every place we go we cannot escape the dust. Inside of our houses, in the laundry, in the latrines, in the mess halls, dust and more dust, dust everywhere."

The other camps were all in places as desolate as Topaz. All were on federally owned land, usually Indian reservations—traditionally the worst land in the U.S. In the new barracks where the prisoners now were housed, each family was supposed to be allowed an "apartment" that measured 20 by 25 feet—a bare room without partitions and no furniture to speak of. But families usually consisted of six or seven members, and often more than one family was crammed into an apartment. No apartment had a stove or running water; each block of 12 or 14 barracks, housing 250 to 300 people, had a community mess hall, laundry, latrines and showers.

The internees worked at tilling the fields to grow food, cooking and serving in the mess halls, collecting garbage.

They manned the police, fire and post office departments for the camps. They published newspapers. They worked as barbers, tailors, cobblers, and candy and magazine vendors. And in spite of the fact that America was treating them like animals in a zoo, they were willing to help in the war effort. They made camouflage nets for the Army, used their talents to paint recruiting posters for the Navy and even conducted experiments in developing artificial rubber for the War Production Board.

No one was allowed any individual profit for his enterprise; a dressmaker was not permitted to make pin money by taking in her neighbor's sewing nor was a jeweler permitted to add to his income by making bracelets or rings for his friends. All work, from cabbage-growing to surgery, was done under the supervision and control of the WRA, which paid the internees $12 a month for unskilled labor, $16 for skilled and $19 for professional work. Sometimes an experienced Japanese doctor earning $19 toiled side by side with a newly graduated Caucasian doctor who earned $500 for doing the same (or less) work.

Though life was bitter, the Japanese-Americans managed to maintain a remarkably stable community life.

Open shower stalls humiliated traditionally modest Japanese women.

Clustering around the stove, a Japanese family celebrates Christmas.

Over four years, the camps were the scenes of 2,120 marriages, 5,981 births and 1,862 deaths from old age. There were nearly 30,000 children of school age among the internees, and though there were not enough books or teachers to go round, the centers managed nevertheless to enroll all the children in classes that met state standards and to graduate 7,220 with high school diplomas. Some centers also ran adult education programs; the one in Topaz had 3,250 grown-ups taking 165 different courses. The two most popular, ironically, were the English language and American history.

Many internment camps continued thus for the duration of the war. Indeed, all of them might have, but for the fact that the WRA, more enlightened than the West Coast racists, had no intention of keeping the prisoners penned up forever. Having got the camps functioning, the WRA moved into a second phase of operation beginning in early 1943 and worked from then on to funnel the prisoners back into the main stream of American life. That was no easy task, for communities that would have them were few and far between. But the WRA persisted, and during the first year found homes and jobs for 17,000 of them. By July 1, 1945, on the eve of Hiroshima, some 55,000 Nisei had been relocated. Many of those who remained in the camps did so voluntarily, from fear of the hostile America on the outside.

Their fears were well founded. When a New Jersey farmer hired five Nisei sent him by the WRA, the town spawned a vigilante committee that set fire to the farm and threatened the life of the farmer's baby. When a Nisei girl who got a job in Denver went to church on Sunday, the minister took her aside and asked, "Wouldn't you feel more at home in your own church?"

Incredibly, almost without exception the young men endured the internment with their faith in the U.S. unimpaired. There were many like Henry Ebihara, who wrote to Secretary of War Henry L. Stimson, saying: "I only ask that I be given a chance to fight to preserve the principles that I have been brought up on and which I will not sacrifice at any cost. Please give me a chance to serve in your armed forces." Eventually 8,000 Nisei did serve —and with great distinction. On January 28, 1943, Stimson announced that the Army would accept Nisei volunteers. They were to be put in segregated units, a fact that most Nisei resented and some suspected was a plot to kill them off. But 1,200 of them signed up from behind the barbed-wire encampments.

They racked up some awesome combat records. No Nisei was ever known to desert from the front lines, though Caucasian unit desertions averaged around 15 per cent. In the Italian campaign the Nisei 442nd Regiment won 3,600 Purple Hearts with 500 Oak Leaf Clusters, 810 Bronze Stars, 342 Silver Stars, 47 Distinguished Service Crosses, 17 Legions of Merit, and a basketful of other citations. Their total casualties, including replacements, were three times their original strength.

In the Pacific they went close enough to enemy lines —at peril of being shot at by both sides—to hear and translate enemy commands. One Nisei serving in Burma, Staff Sergeant Kenny Yasui, called "Baby Sergeant York" for his small size, posed as a Japanese colonel, strode up to 13 Japanese soldiers, smartly gave them orders in their own language, and marched them, unsuspecting, back to his own commander, having taken them all as prisoners.

After the war, the Nisei were able to step back into the regular life of U.S. civilians, managing for the most part to leave behind the bitterness and hurt of the years inside barbed wire. Unhappily, no such easy adjustment awaited the loyal but weary Issei. The majority of them were too old to start new lives even if they had not felt spiritually defeated. Facing the bleak aftermath of nearly four years' internment, they felt overwhelming despair. Their feelings were summed up by Akana Imamura, one of their number, who wrote: "The life of most of us Issei is now well spent. We stand in the evening of life where there is no hope. . . . We are told and encouraged to relocate again into the world as a stranger in strange communities! We now have lost all security. WRA urges readjustment, relocating outside. Where shall we go? What shall we do at the twilight of the evening of our lives?"

On a subzero morning at a Wyoming relocation center, Nisei internees, led by a Boy Scout drum-and-bugle corps, salute the American flag.

After the War

Home from Europe just after V-E Day, a jubilant airman kisses U.S. soil.

The Readjustment

Has Your Husband come home to the right woman?
LADIES' HOME JOURNAL, 1945

Every serviceman had his own image of what he was going to do when he got home. Some swore they would grab the first girl they saw, and did *(right)*. Others planned to sleep for a month, getting up only for edible, home-cooked meals. Others planned to blow their separation pay on the longest binge of their lives.

But after a few days or weeks of living out such fantasies, the hero had to face up to some hard facts—how he would get a job and where he would live.

Because of wartime priorities, few new civilian dwellings had been built during the preceding years. The government had promised 2.7 million new houses by 1948, but meanwhile President Truman begged the public to find living space for veterans. The city of Atlanta bought 100 trailers for married GIs; in North Dakota, veterans turned surplus grain bins into housing; in Cleveland, Benny Goodman's band played for a benefit at which citizens pledged rooms for rent, instead of money.

Getting a job turned out to be less of a problem than many had anticipated. Some veterans set up their own businesses with government loans and money they had saved in the service. Others returned to their old trades or went to college on the more than $500 yearly tuition plus living allowance ($90 a month for married men) provided by a generous law called the GI Bill of Rights. Although some veterans would always bear physical and emotional scars from the war, most were quickly caught up in the new America they discovered—the gadgets like television, the new personalities in politics and entertainment and the new fads *(following pages)*.

But there were many people—psychologists, sociologists and just plain mothers and wives—who were determined to believe in a readjustment problem, and to solve it. Articles ran in women's magazines with titles like "What You Can Do to Help the Returning Veteran" and "Will He Be Changed?" *Good Housekeeping* said: "After two or three weeks he should be finished with talking, with oppressive remembering. If he still goes over the same stories, reveals the same emotions, you had best consult a psychiatrist. This condition is neurotic." *House Beautiful* suggested that "Home must be the greatest rehabilitation center of them all" and photographed a living room designed for a returning general. The editors also noted that Wacs and Waves, starved for feminine frills, would expect their bedrooms to be redecorated. "G.I. Jane," they solemnly stated, "will retool with ruffles."

In Times Square, a sailor grabs a girl and celebrates in his own fashion, V-J Day, August 14, 1945—the end of the war with Japan.

After the War

Shopping for civvies, a soldier sizes up a sharp, double-breasted suit; after discharge, soldiers had 30 days before they had to get out of uniform and into civilian clothes.

As the services demobilized, every discharged GI was awarded this bronze lapel button decorated with a spread eagle, irreverently dubbed "the ruptured duck."

Hubert Humphrey, elected Senator from Minnesota in November 1948, grasps tools given him by a friend with the note: "Be on the square and keep hammering away." At the Democratic National Convention Humphrey had jammed through a liberal civil-rights plank in the party platform. ▶

In "The Best Years of Our Lives," the movie of 1946, the disabled veteran was played by Harold Russell, a former paratrooper whose hands had been blown off on D-Day.

The question at left introduced the home permanent to millions of women in 1947. Later the Federal Trade Commission revealed that although one of the girls had indeed given herself a home wave, both had subsequently gone to a hairdresser.

Penicillin, produced by molds like the one pictured in this laboratory dish, was first used by the military during the war; later it became available to civilians as well. ▶

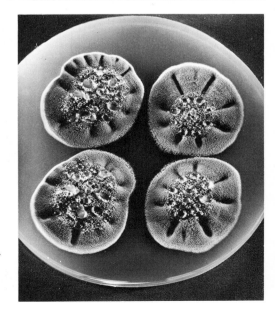

◀ *Betty MacDonald gazes at the subject of her book "The Egg and I." This and the other top sellers of 1945 and 1946, listed below, reflect a postwar taste for escapism.*

FOREVER AMBER

THE ROBE

THE BLACK ROSE

BRAVE MEN

DEAR SIR

THE KING'S GENERAL

THIS SIDE OF INNOCENCE

THE RIVER ROAD

PEACE OF MIND

AS HE SAW IT

"Don't Mind Me—Just Go Right On Talking"

▲
Eden Ahbez, composer of 1948's hit tune "Nature Boy" (below) and a conspicuous ascetic, meditates on his success in the natural environment of a cool canyon stream.

THERE WAS A BOY,

A VERY STRANGE, ENCHANTED BOY . . .

A LITTLE SHY AND SAD OF EYE,

BUT VERY WISE WAS HE . . .

THIS HE SAID TO ME:

"THE GREATEST THING

YOU'LL EVER LEARN

IS JUST TO LOVE

AND BE LOVED IN RETURN."

Milton Berle was one of the regiment of▶ vaudevillians who were rescued from oblivion by TV. As host of "The Texaco Star Theater," Berle sang, danced, did imitations and mugged—and earned $6,500 a week and the informal title of "Mr. Television."

Mrs. Clyde Smith grabs the loot she has won in a Pyramid Club. A craze in 1949, the clubs required members to pay, say, one dollar each, and recruit two others at a dollar a head. After 12 days a member theoretically won $2,048—but most clubs folded because of the decreasing mathematical probability of finding new members.

Loafing at a Long Island soda shop, ex-GIs enjoy their membership in the "52-20 Club" named for the unemployment pay of $20 for 52 weeks granted discharged servicemen. By August 1946, six million had drawn an average of two months' benefits and General Omar Bradley, Veterans Administrator, began worrying that the boys would never get back to work. ▼

▲ *A busy carhop serves refreshments to moviegoers at one of the 2,000 drive-ins built across the country between 1947 and 1950.*

Republican Senators Arthur Vandenberg (left) and Robert Taft plan their opposition to Truman. Vandenberg dominated foreign affairs while Taft led domestic legislation. ▼

▲

Vibrant Ava Gardner emerged as Hollywood's sexiest star when she appeared in films like "The Hucksters" and "Wanted."

Ed Gardner of radio's "Duffy's Tavern" started each program on the phone: "Duffy's Tavern. . . . Archie the manager speaking. Duffy ain't here. Oh, hello Duffy."

In 1950 United Nations negotiator Ralph ▶ Bunche became the first Negro to win the Nobel Peace Prize. Bunche received the $31,674 award for bringing an end to the Arab-Israeli war, which had broken out in major fighting on May 15, 1948.

During the fad for goopy delights like the one below, Americans gobbled up a record 714 million gallons of ice cream in 1946. ▼

By 1949 Americans were buying 100,000 ▶ television sets a week. Quiz shows and soap operas were favored by the chorebound.

TV hero to those under 13 was cowboy Hopalong Cassidy, played by William Boyd. He became so popular that "Hoppy" clothing grossed $40 million by 1950. ▼

Bob Hope solos without benefit of aircraft when catapulted from a tree in one of his first postwar films, "The Paleface."

The 1948 Presidential election was the first to be shown on mass TV. The tally on the TV screen at right indicates the narrow margin by which Truman upset Dewey.

"Madman" Muntz reigned as postwar king of used-car dealers, holding to list prices to compete with a booming black market.

Congressman Richard Nixon fires a question during the 1948 hearings involving ex-State Department official Alger Hiss.

Though he earned almost a million dollars in 1950 as a radio and TV announcer, Arthur Godfrey often loathed commercials, as he made clear (below) during plugs. But his folksy banter prompted Fred Allen to call him "the man with the barefoot voice."

HOUSING SHORTAGE

NO VACANCIES

"BE IT EVER SO HUMBLE"

THE KINSEY REPORT

Dr. Alfred C. Kinsey interviews one of the 5,300 American men whose intimate lives he explored for his 1948 bestseller, "Sexual Behavior in the Human Male." Some of his startling findings are listed below.

SEXUAL ACTIVITY AND MARRIAGE
85 per cent of married men have had pre-marital sex and 50 per cent are unfaithful.

SEXUAL ACTIVITY BY AGE
95 per cent of all males are active by 15, and maximum activity occurs at 16 or 17.

SEXUAL ACTIVITY BY OCCUPATION
Semi-skilled laborers are the most active group, men in the professions second, day laborers third, white collar workers last.

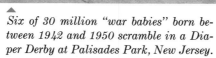

Six of 30 million "war babies" born between 1942 and 1950 scramble in a Diaper Derby at Palisades Park, New Jersey.

◄ Seated amid 10 years of scripts, Gertrude Berg, star and creator of the daytime serial "The Goldbergs," beams as her show graduates from radio to television in 1948. As Molly Goldberg, the Jewish mother, Gertrude Berg began every show leaning out of her window schmoozing with neighbors. Typical Goldbergisms: "Enter, whoever" and "If it's nobody, I'll call back."

The inventor of the LP, Dr. Peter Goldmark, holds a pile of 33-rpm records containing all the music in the eight-foot tower of old 78-rpm recordings at right. ▶

Progressive Party Presidential candidate Henry Wallace grabs a quick bite during his 1948 campaign. A fourth party, the Dixiecrats, ran Strom Thurmond. Both mavericks finished far behind Truman and Dewey.

The return of new cars after the war is symbolized by the showroom appearance of the 1947 Frazer. Its manufacturer, Kaiser-Frazer, was the first new company to make American cars in more than 20 years.

Lithuanians arrive in America. By 1950, some 200,000 D.P.s had come to the U.S.

In 1949 Russell Lynes, editor of "Harper's Magazine," divided the nation into three intellectual categories: highbrow, lowbrow and middlebrow. "Life" magazine then posed three representatives of Lynes's thesis in characteristic plumage and habitat (above). Each dressed in the clothes of his cultural station, a highbrow (left) contemplates a Picasso, a lowbrow looks at calendar art and a middlebrow studies a Grant Wood reproduction.

When his suppertime TV show for kids began, Howdy Doody sang his theme song.

IT'S HOWDY DOODY TIME.
IT'S HOWDY DOODY TIME.
BOB SMITH AND HOWDY TOO
SAY HOWDY-DOO TO YOU.

The first Negro to be admitted to the University of Arkansas Medical School, Edith Mae Irby waits for a class to begin while white students try to be casual about the tense moment. Miss Irby's admission in 1949 marked the beginning of sustained efforts to integrate colleges in the South.

◀ Warren Austin, America's first representative to the United Nations, stands between the flags of the U.S. and the U.N.

Razzing his own product, radio comedian ▶ Henry Morgan dons earmuffs to silence the deafening racket of a breakfast cereal he is advertising. Zany and enormously popular, Morgan interviewed himself, alienated several sponsors, once auctioned off his entire radio executive staff for $83.

◀ Typical of a rash of postwar girlie promotion stunts is the coronation of Barbara Hendricks of New York as "Miss Grill" for serving up 600 frankfurters in one hour.

The Senate's vituperative racist, Theodore Bilbo, who wanted all Negroes deported to Liberia, called on "every redblooded white man to use any means to keep the niggers away from the polls."
▼

After the War

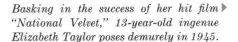

Singing commercials inundated the nation's postwar radio audience. "Chiquita Banana," a calypso-beat product booster, was sung 2,700 times a week at one point. The Pepsi-Cola jingle (below) was another postwar favorite, though written in 1939.

PEPSI COLA HITS THE SPOT,
TWELVE FULL OUNCES, THAT'S A LOT,
TWICE AS MUCH FOR A NICKEL TOO,
PEPSI COLA IS THE DRINK FOR YOU!
NICKEL, NICKEL, NICKEL, NICKEL,
TRICKLE, TRICKLE, TRICKLE, TRICKLE,
NICKEL, NICKEL, NICKEL, NICKEL!

Basking in the success of her hit film ▶ *"National Velvet," 13-year-old ingenue Elizabeth Taylor poses demurely in 1945.*

Addressing the Democrats' Jefferson-Jackson Day dinner in Washington in 1948, Harry Truman, a strong advocate of civil rights, faced a table that had been reserved for—but left conspicuously empty by—segregationist Southern Democrats.

The biggest GI on any campus, Dwight Eisenhower pauses beside his wife Mamie and son John during Ike's inauguration in 1948 as president of Columbia University. Ike was one of half a million veterans who went to college after the war was over. ▶

220

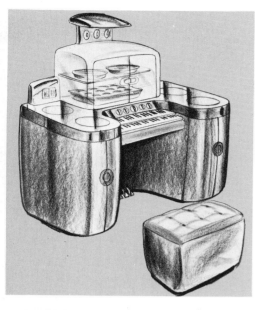

This musical stove was a purely fanciful contraption that cooked food only when its piano was played. It was created by Jean O. Reinecke—inventor of a real gadget, the electric guitar—as part of a magazine feature spoofing the boom in household machinery. The electric clothes drier was first marketed in 1946; by 1950 some 750,000 garbage disposal units had been sold, and automatic dishwashers were being purchased at a rate of 225,000 a year.

Running for his first political office, 29-year-old John F. Kennedy relaxes under his campaign poster in 1946. Kennedy won election to the House by 78,000 votes. ▶

▲
Emcee Dave Garroway ducks cotton baseballs hurled by the cast of his Chicago-based music and comedy show after he had slurred Chicago's last-place Cubs in 1949.

◀ With impassioned rhetoric, an up-and-coming evangelist named Billy Graham exhorts a crowd in Los Angeles to repent. Graham burst upon California—and the nation—in 1949 when he drew more than 300,000 people into his Los Angeles tent and converted 6,000 of them—including one notorious gangster, one cowboy singer and track star Louis Zamperini.

Moody Marlon Brando, shown tootling a ▶ recorder, was hailed in 1947 as Broadway's best young actor for his performance in "A Streetcar Named Desire."

A left hook by Joe Louis sends Billy Conn to the canvas.

The End of the Long Wait

We shall miss the chaotic performances of 1945, the disorder and confusion. It will be much better baseball that we will see this year but we doubt whether it will prove either as interesting or exciting as the low-grade product of 1945.

SPORTS COLUMNIST H.G. SALSINGER, 1946

Through four long years of war, American sports fans, like American wives and sweethearts, waited for their heroes to return. In their minds were the images of departed stars—a young, lean Joe DiMaggio awaiting his next time at bat; a sleek Joe Louis stalking a challenger. But before their eyes, in wartime sports arenas, lurched a crew of has-beens and never-would-be's whose big-league incumbency was an exercise in heroic malfeasance.

Things were so bad that in the fall of 1945 sports writer Warren Brown, in assessing the two clubs that had stumbled into the World Series, predicted "I don't believe *either* team can win."

Then in 1946 the pros came back, and once again all seemed right with the sports world. Joe DiMaggio, flecks of gray now showing in his slicked-back hair, slugged 25 home runs that year. Stan Musial won the National League batting title and helped carry the Cardinals into the World Series. And Joe Louis, noting just before his long-awaited return bout with Billy Conn that the elusive challenger "can run but he can't hide," came through with the expected knockout.

While all the old heroes seemed satisfactorily the same, the games to which they returned were changing. The tra-ditionally white-man's world of organized baseball got its first Negro *(pages 230-233)*. The U.S. baseball industry also got its first big scare in a long time when a Mexican millionaire named Jorge Pasquel raided the majors for talent in an abortive effort to start his own big league in Mexico. Pasquel was quickly defeated by a counterfire of U.S. dollars. But at this same time the powerful National Football League found itself faced by a very healthy new-born rival named the All-America Football Conference, which wooed players with such success that in 1950 the old league agreed to a merger.

The most important new influence on sport, however, was television. Mike Jacobs, boxing's top impresario, prophesied that title bouts would be held in empty studios for the cameras only. Many baseball and football executives agreed. Yet it soon became obvious that TV was not killing off the live fan, but rather creating a new generation of sports lovers. In 1948 the Cleveland Indians drew over 2.5 million fans, the largest gate ever for a single season. By decade's end, pro football had doubled its attendance, and boxers like middleweights Tony Zale and Rocky Graziano were fighting for purses that men their size had never touched in the days before television.

Graceful even in repose, Joe DiMaggio kneels in Yankee Stadium's on-deck circle in 1941, the year he hit safely in 56 consecutive games.

Cocking his arm, Chicago Cardinal tailback Ron Cahill displays the crisp form that produced 21 interceptions in but 109 attempted passes.

A Galaxy of Goofballs

In an effort to keep professional sports alive during the war, major-league promoters reached down into the misty mid-regions of mediocrity for any lukewarm body that could fill a uniform. The National Football League lumped what was left of the Pittsburgh Steelers and the Philadelphia Eagles into one dreadful crew nicknamed the Steagles. In baseball, the Cincinnati Reds brought up a gangly, 15-year-old pitcher named Joe Nuxhall. A sampling of other performers from the nonvintage war years is shown here, along with the atrocious records they set.

Boston Red Sox first baseman George Metkovich, shown embracing his catcher—not the ball—committed three errors in a single inning.

Gallant but cruelly handicapped, one-armed Pete Gray was a starting left-fielder and leadoff batter in the order for the St. Louis Browns.

New York Rangers goalie Ken McAuley, seen above at a much-needed practice, allowed 15 goals in one game against the Detroit Red Wings.

New York Giant outfielder—and clown—Danny Gardella was informed at war's end that "players of his type would no longer be needed."

Philadelphia Phillies manager Fred Fitzsimmons proudly surveys his starting line-up. Star of the team, known as the Phutile Phillies, was

fat Jimmie Foxx (second from left), who was coaxed out of retirement "to help the club." He did—to 16 consecutive losses in May and June.

Big Noise at the Ballpark

Almost everyone thought that the owners of the mighty New York Yankees had taken leave of their senses when, in October 1948, they hired Charles Dillon (Casey) Stengel to manage their club. During his playing days, Casey's principal reputation had been as a clown; once he tipped his cap to booing fans and a sparrow flew out. Later, as the unsuccessful manager of several talent-poor teams, he was described by a writer in *The Sporting News* as the funniest pilot in the game.

Casey, a little awed at first by his prestigious job, cheerfully conceded that the Yankees' great personnel left him no excuse for losing. "I never had good ones like this before," he said. He then proceeded to juggle those players so skillfully that, despite injuries to such key men as Joe DiMaggio and Tommy Henrich, the Yankees won the 1949 pennant and shortly thereafter celebrated *(right)* a victory in the World Series. To the delight of Yankee fans, the irrepressible Casey repeated these triumphs the following year. He also delighted journalists during interviews by his ability to juggle the English language in a roundabout, non-stop jargon, half nonsense and half horse sense, that became known throughout the sports world as Stengelese.

Now the reason this club hasn't made a deal is why should we? When you got players good enough to win a pennant on the road and a World Series on the road which is where they win the majority of their games and against a tree-mendous club like this one which you know is a great ball club because why have they played us more games in the World Series than anybody, then why would you want to change? . . . Now age from your pitchers can kill and you ask about the shortstop, but those young fellows can whip you if they get careless. Some of these men get reading the papers how great they are and think that's it, but that's phony, they don't throw you the same ball up there every day. And whenever I make a deal I get swindled.

STENGEL ON BASEBALL TRADES

Casey Stengel whoops it up with Yankee owners and players in the locker room after winning the 1949 World Series over the Brooklyn Dodgers.

229

"If You Were Only White"

"Many a shepherd of a limping major club has made no secret of his yearning to trade more than a couple of buttsprung outfielders for colored players of the calibre of Satchel Paige," TIME magazine reported in 1940. But there was no chance in that era of Jim Crow that any such trade would be made. Baseball, like most other major American team sports, had been lily-white since its founding days. None of the front-office men was going to risk offending the customers by putting a Negro player on the roster, no matter how good he might be.

Yet Leroy "Satchel" (short for Satchelfoot) Paige, along with dozens of other colored athletes, had more than enough talent to make any man's ball club—as both the big-league owners and their white players discovered in off-season exhibition games. After one such exhibition in

---

SATCHEL'S RULES FOR GOOD LIVING

1. *Avoid fried foods which angry up the blood.*
2. *If your stomach disputes you, pacify it with cool thoughts.*
3. *Keep the juices flowing by jangling around gently as you move.*
4. *Go very light on the vices, such as carrying on in society, as the social ramble ain't restful.*
5. *Avoid running at all times.*
6. *Don't look back, something might be gaining on you.*

---

which Paige mowed down a row of white sluggers, Dizzy Dean, premier pitcher for the St. Louis Cardinals, declared "Satchelfoot is worth $200,000 in any big league's money." This comment came at a time when Dean himself was paid perhaps a tenth of that.

Even as it was, Paige probably made as much as the richest white stars. Though by necessity he played most of his games in the scrubby Negro leagues, barnstorming the year round from one ramshackle stadium to another, Satch was able to parlay his enormous talents both as a player and a promoter into an income as high as $50,000 a year. The other colored stars, however, played for pea-

nuts—flavored with dubious compliments prefaced by: "If you were only white."

Ironically, when the shifting racial climate of postwar America prompted major-league teams to begin hiring Negroes, it was not Paige who got the first call. That role was thrust upon a college-bred athlete named Jackie Robinson by Branch Rickey, shrewd general manager of the Brooklyn Dodgers. Rickey, who mixed a tinge of social evangelism with his baseball sense, was determined that his chosen Negro succeed not only as an outstanding ballplayer but as an exemplary character. Robinson had a reputation as an athlete with an explosive temper. To test his man, in their first interview Rickey suddenly called Robinson "Nigger!" He followed with a string of other ugly comments and wound up by kicking the startled athlete in the shin. Robinson kept his temper—and Rickey signed him to play for the Dodgers.

During his first season, Robinson's restraint was again tested—the St. Louis Cardinals, for example, threatened a boycott and one Cardinal tossed a black cat onto the field one day while Robinson was playing. But when the year was over, the Cardinals, who had been favored to win the pennant, were in second place; Brooklyn led the league, and Jackie Robinson, who had batted .297, was named Rookie of the Year.

With that triumph, the old barriers crashed down. The following season the major leagues had a half-dozen Negro stars, one of whom was none other than the old barnstormer himself, Satchel Paige. Though he was by now at least 40 (no one was ever sure), Paige quickly proved he had not lost his touch either as a pitcher or as a promoter. Upon signing his contract, he was asked if he thought he was capable of pitching day after day against major-league sluggers. Paige replied, "Plate's still the same size," then proceeded, in a half-season, to win six games while losing but one, helping the Cleveland Indians to a pennant. And Paige won himself thousands of additional fans through skillful manipulation of his assumed role as the wise black gypsy whose six rules for life (*above, left*) were guaranteed to bring anyone to a happy old age.

Satchel Paige rests before a game. Told he might be named Rookie of the Year, Paige replied, "Twenty-two years is a long time to be a rookie."

Plunging into third base, Jackie Robinson, first Negro to make the big leagues, flashes the aggressive skill that made him Rookie of the Year in 1947.

Though the color bar in football was never so oppressive as in baseball—Negroes had starred for decades on mixed college teams—the colored footballer did not make it big in the pro game until a small group of exceptionally gifted players, led by Marion Motley *(right)*, burst onto the field in 1946. Fittingly, the arrival of the Negro in the big time was bound up with the fortunes of a Johnny-come-lately team, the Cleveland Browns of the All-America Football Conference, just established as a rival to the National Football League. Motley joined the Browns and proved to be the prototype of a new kind of fullback. He weighed a bone-crunching 238 pounds; he was also remarkably shifty, allowing him to elude some tacklers while flattening others. Furthermore, his ferocious blocking made passing a safe pastime for quarterback Otto Graham. The Browns won four consecutive championships in the All-America Conference. Then, in 1949, the AAC concluded a merger agreement with the National Football League under which the Browns—and several other teams —were absorbed into the older organization. Their induction was accompanied by a barrage of disparaging remarks from NFL fans, who claimed the Browns would now learn how pro ball was really played.

But it was quickly evident that Motley and the other Browns already knew. In their first NFL season, 1950, they won the championship of their division. Unimpressed, their detractors said the real test would come in the play-off game against the other division champions, the powerful Los Angeles Rams. When the big game got under way the Rams delighted old NFL fans by scoring a touchdown in just 27 seconds. The Browns fought back, but with only one minute and 48 seconds left to play, they were behind 28-27 and pinned back on their own 32-yard line. Protected by Motley's ponderous blocking, Graham raced the clock downfield to the Rams' 16. There, with 20 seconds left, a field goal made the upstart Cleveland team the champions of the football world. And on top of that world sat Marion Motley: the leader among pro runners with 810 yards gained for the season, and the unanimous choice as the NFL's all-star fullback.

Browns fullback Marion Motley sweeps end against Pittsburgh in 1950. In this game he set a club record by averaging 17.09 yards per carry.

A sharp-shooting ring master, Sugar Ray Robinson slams a long right to the kidney as he easily overcomes a bobbing, weaving Kid Gavilan.

Boxing's Life Masters

Rarely had there been as many first-rate fighters plying their brutal trade as during the closing years of the '40s. From gentlemanly Joe Louis, model king of the heavyweights, down to pasty-faced featherweight Willie Pep, master of the blacker arts of the prize ring, virtually every division boasted not only an outstanding champion but a formidable list of challengers. Pep, for example, fought arch-rival Sandy Saddler in a series of battles that promised to stand through eternity as textbook examples of not only how to box but also how to knee, gouge, spin, grab, heel, backhand and butt while still remaining technically within the rules.

But it was the medium-sized fighters who put on the most attractive displays of premeditated violence. Dominating the welterweights was lithe, handsome Walker Smith, a graduate of the Harlem streets whose stubborn pride on such matters as segregated facilities earned him a hasty discharge from the U.S. armed forces. Under the boxing *nom de guerre* of Sugar Ray Robinson, he rolled through his bouts with such consummate ease that he was suspected of toying with even his most dangerous opponents. A New York sports writer remarked after one of Robinson's masterful, but notably restrained, performances that the champion "appeared to be round-shouldered from holding up the challenger." In the 14th round of another title defense, against flashy Kid Gavilan, Sugar Ray was so confidently in command *(left)* that he stuck out his tongue at ringsider Joe Louis, who had picked Gavilan to win. And to the erstwhile street urchin, it all seemed so easy. "Boxing's simple," he explained. "The other man can't hit you with but one hand at a time. And you got your right hand free to block that. And that leaves your own left hand free to hit him any way you want."

Such mastery of the complex science totally escaped the most exciting middleweight of the era, a wild street brawler named Rocky Graziano, who had spent part of his adolescence in solitary confinement as an incorrigible and had lost several of his boyhood friends to various forms of sudden death—including the electric chair. While being built up for a title bout in a series of matches against smaller men, Rocky explained his technique thus: "I eat up welterweights." And indeed, he did *(below)*. Then he went in against middleweight champion Tony Zale and discovered that in boxing's jungle, everybody was likely to get eaten. Through a series of three bouts that had never been equalled for sheer ferocity in the prize ring, Rocky was knocked out; then he, in turn, knocked out Zale to become champion; and finally Rocky was demolished once again in a donnybrook that led to his retirement. Even in his one winning bout with Zale, Graziano was so battered that in the ritual post-fight interview, the best thoughts he could muster were: "What? what? what? Yeah, yeah, yeah. It's marvelous. It's marvelous."

Inelegant but effective, Rocky Graziano demolishes Charley Fusari.

On September 27, 1950, boxing fans received an emotional jolt from which many of them would never quite recover *(below)*. In Yankee Stadium Joe Louis, who had retired after 12 years in which he never lost a bout as heavyweight champion, returned to the ring wars against Ezzard Charles. That night, Joe was a sad, distant cry from the catlike destroyer whose knockout punch had mowed down opponents with such terrible, swift regularity that his title defenses had become known as "The Bum of the Month Parade." Now, the erstwhile Brown Bomber was old (36) and fat (218), and a bald spot gleamed discouragingly un-der the klieg lights. Yet sentimental spectators had swallowed the myth that Charles was only a light heavyweight who had been beefed up for the event; and they hoped that Joe would somehow win—as he always had.

It was a forlorn hope, for Charles in reality was a superb, slashing boxer. He quickly took charge, and on his way to an easy, 15-round decision, had Louis holding onto the ring ropes in the 14th round. Asked later why he had not knocked out Louis then and there, Charles, a modest and notably honest man, said of his boyhood idol, "When I saw that great man helpless, I just couldn't do it."

To at least one observer, it seemed that men who sadly watched the humiliation of Joe Louis last week in Yankee Stadium were really feeling sorry for themselves. So many, in the uncomfortably long span of Louis's greatness, had themselves picked up fortyish weight and lost twentyish confidence since the first night they saw him come into New York and Yankee Stadium. And anything they felt may have been made more acute by the fact that Louis's story, in its major phase, began and ended on the same spot: the Stadium's garishly lighted, 20-by-20-foot patch of canvas. There in 1935 he had instantly excited them with their first look at his terribly swift hands, made to seem swifter by his own shuffling deliberateness and the ponderous immensity of his foe, Primo Carnera. There, only a year later, Max Schmeling found the flaw and gave him his first beating. Later Schmeling said the kid would never be able to forget it, and in a way he was right. In 1938, the German was shipped from the Stadium to a hospital after just two minutes and 4 seconds of exposure to the kid's rage.

At the Stadium, ten years later, the world heavyweight championship's longest possessor (eleven years, eight months) and most willing defender (25 bouts) preceded his retirement with one more knockout (his 51st in 61 fights). Last week, pressed for cash to settle an income-tax bill, he paid the Stadium one more visit (and made $102,840). . . .

For moments in the fourth and tenth rounds, Louis's left shot out with some of its remembered cobra sureness if not much of its quickness; the right followed with something of the full, overhand pitch that had rubbled so many men. He shut up Charles's left eye. But Charles turned Louis's face into a puffed, bloody lump and made him grab a ring rope in the fourteenth round to avoid falling. As a man with little experience in taking beatings (two in seventeen professional years), Louis took this one well, stubbornly marching into it. Yet referee Mark Conn could give the old champion no more than five rounds. One judge gave Charles twelve rounds; the other handed him thirteen.

A few young bloods wondered if Charles, belittled before this victory, mightn't have licked Louis the best day he ever saw. Charles himself indicated that it would take more than an hour's work (i.e., fifteen of his best rounds) to make that talk make sense. "I want to be a credit to the ring," he told an estimated television audience of 25,000,000, "just like the great champion I beat tonight." NEWSWEEK, OCTOBER 9, 1950

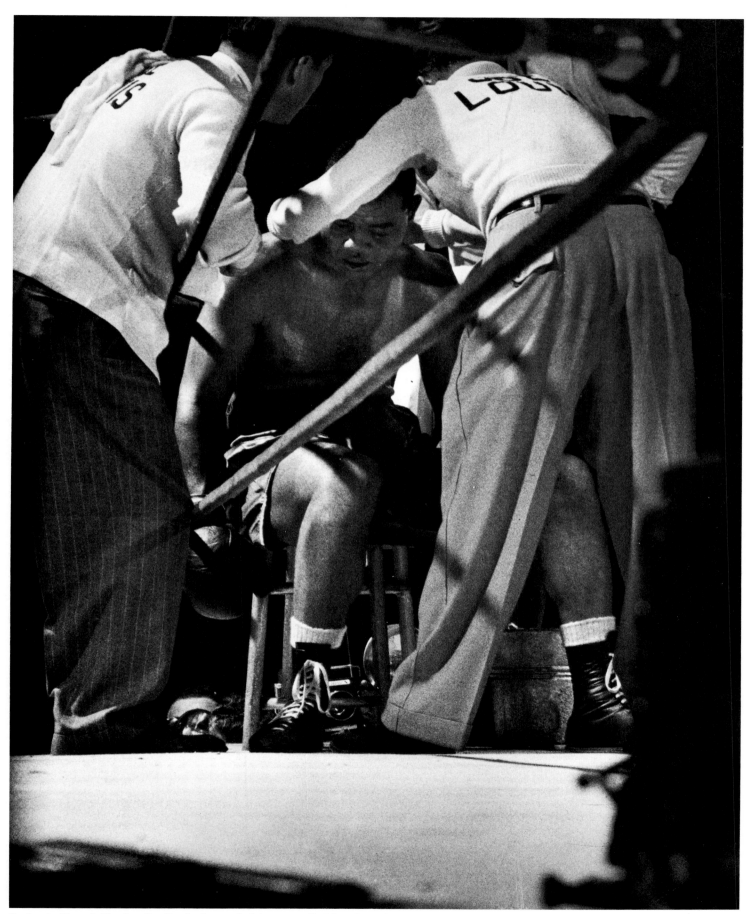

Losing to Ezzard Charles, Joe Louis slumps in his corner. Stricken fans of Louis claimed this was not the real Joe, only "what was left of him."

Gaudy Star of the Electronic Side Show

During the sports boom of the very late '40s the new medium, television, in an effort to fill the dead spots between boxing bouts and big-league ball games, began to serve up a side show of quasi-sports such as Roller Derby and professional wrestling. To everyone's astonishment, these oddball exhibitions prospered—and returned the favor by helping to spank the infant TV to a lucrative life. In fact, one of their demi-heroes, a hunk of peroxided beefcake named Gorgeous George, became one of television's first celebrities. Though a few easy-going sports writers were delighted at the pre-match antics (*excerpted below*) of Gorgeous George, traditionalists like Red Smith of the *New York Herald Tribune* were outraged: "Groucho Marx is prettier," sputtered Smith in 1949, "Sonny Tufts a more gifted actor, Connie Mack a better rassler and the Princeton Triangle Club has far superior female impersonators." In the face of such slings, George grunted and groaned all the way to the bank; he grossed $70,000 per season.

Gorgeous George's valet enters the ring. Tonight it's Jackson, a small, baldheaded man in a tail coat and green vest. He is carrying, reverently, a large silver tray, on which rests a small folded prayer-rug, a yellow towel with a large GG monogram in the center, a chromium-plated spray gun, and an atomizer or two. Setting down the tray, he takes the shiny gun and SPRAYS the entire ring with scented and antiseptic toilet water to remove all germs, sweat smells, and other obnoxious remnants.

Then he places the small prayer-rug at the side of the ring where George is to enter, brushes it off with a whiskbroom, and stands beside it at attention. By this time the excitement is pretty tense, with much confused babble and neck-craning.

Then, "There he comes! He's in PINK tonight!" And Gorgeous comes striding slowly down the aisle. He is indeed in pink. He has on a pink satin quilted robe, with a lining of yellow silk, and sequin epaulets. George has 88 of them, including several of ermine. Knotted loosely at his throat is a scarf of salmon-colored silk. His hair, a mass of golden ringlets, looks as though he has just spent four hours in a beauty parlor. George makes the grand entrance, sneering at the peons. Slowly and calmly he removes his Georgie pins—gold-plated and sequined bobby pins—and casts them to the crowd. And shakes out his hair like a lordly spaniel. HANNIBAL COONS, *SPORT* MAGAZINE, *1949*

Just before a big match, George proudly waits out a permanent wave.

Daintily peeling off a hairnet, Jackson, the valet, unleashes George's gorgeous mane while the master busies himself with his fur-trimmed silk robe.

Freewheeling Brawl

In 1935 marathon-dance impresario Leo Seltzer gloomily counted the dwindling house and decided to find some other way to make a living. Casting wildly about, he hooked a bunch of roller skaters and convinced them that people would pay hard cash to watch them race around a track and crash into each other. Seltzer dubbed the dubious show the Roller Derby and began barnstorming. For over 10 years, attendance at the Roller Derby was awful. Then Seltzer talked his way into television. By 1949 thousands of Americans were hunkering down happily in their living rooms to watch the fast-moving brawlers. Naturally, conservative sports fans had no more use for the Roller Derby than for wrestling. "The Roller Derby is a sport," wrote John Lardner, with deep sarcasm. "Defenestration is also a sport, for those who like it."

On the attack, a Roller Derby girl tries to muscle past two blockers.

Haranguing two hapless foes she has sent sprawling, Derby star Gerry Murray gets a round of delighted applause from a passing teammate.

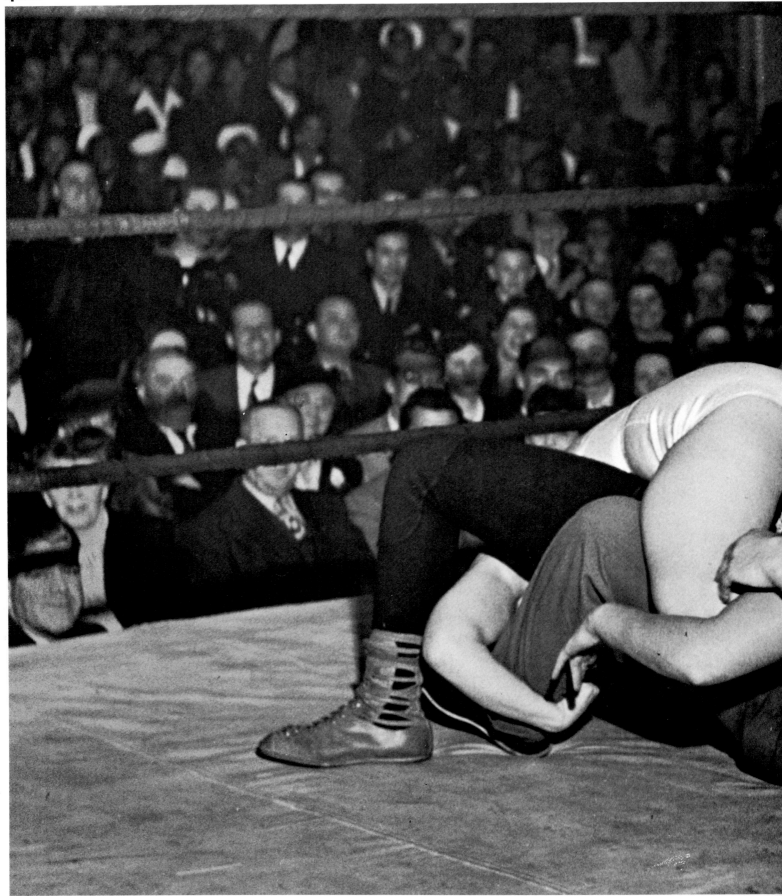

Low man in a writhing tangle of bodies, a referee tries to disengage two lady grapplers. Wrestling fans relished such contrived shenanigans.

Fashion

Top models pose languidly in classic '40s styles.

The Distant Drum

If American women humiliate themselves by following these imbecilic fashion changes like a herd of ludicrous cattle, their twentieth-century emancipation is just an empty boast.   THE REVEREND DR. A. POWELL DAVIES, WASHINGTON, D.C., 1947

Before the war, the American fashion world had never tried to stand on its own creative legs. Though homegrown garment designers and manufacturers ran a three-billion-dollar industry in the U.S., they always trusted Paris to tell them what styles to create, what fabrics to use and where to place buttons and beads. But when the fashion oracles in Paris were suddenly shut off by the war, Americans had to make all these crucial decisions themselves—for the first time.

If this were not agony enough, government regulation L-85 strictly limited the fabric a civilian manufacturer might use: no more than two inches of hem; no more than one patch-pocket per blouse; no attached hoods or shawls; no skirt more than 72 inches around; no belts more than two inches wide; no cuffs on coats.

Faced with this awesome challenge, the local talent and its promoters, the lady editors of sleek fashion magazines, performed what were modestly confessed to be a succession of miracles, such as the convertible costume on *Vogue's* cover, right. At the slip of its daytime jacket, the soft blouse and skirt became an ensemble either for dining out or for an evening of informal dancing. "Zingo," said *Harper's Bazaar* proudly of its own almost identical

discoveries: "Proof that American ingenuity makes of shortages not makeshifts but new worlds."

With their chins up pertly, these glossy magazines kept coming on with a seemingly endless supply of such wisps of escape fantasy for women at war. For example, in its February 15, 1944, issue *Vogue* bubbled brightly: "Spring. It is unreasonable, irrepressible, ridiculous—and wonderful. It may be a new cutaway suit—or an old suit with a new shantung blouse. Whatever you may be doing, short of hoeing your Victory Garden #3, you may be . . . quite correctly be . . . wearing a suit."

That message, and others like it, got across; for four years American women happily bought the spartan suits, skimpy skirts, and unpocketed, ruffleless blouses. Then, with war's end, a heavy blow fell from the gossamer pages of the fashion magazines. In newly freed Paris, an unknown French couturier named Christian Dior showed a collection of dresses styled in direct opposition to all the American ideas the slick fashion press had been touting. Without turning a hair on their shiny heads, *Vogue, Bazaar, Glamour* and the rest announced that all yesterday's clothes were absolutely out of date and from now on women could only wear the exciting, Parisian "New Look."

GLAMOUR

Harper's BAZAAR

August 1947

VOGUE

OUR
RATION-AL
LIVES
New Possibilities in
FOOD—CLOTHES
and TRANSPORTATION
in line with
wartime rationing

APRIL 15, 1942
PRICE 35 CENTS
40 CENTS IN CANADA

Decrees the Hidden Leg

In late 1945, less than a year after the last German had decamped, a middle-aged Parisian named Christian Dior sat down and sketched out a handful of outrageously luxuriant dresses. With their swirling skirts 12 inches from the floor, shoulders definitely without padding and bosoms definitely with, they changed every wartime fashion notion that America had so conscientiously observed.

When Dior's creations went on display at his Paris salon, American fashion-magazine editors in the audience went into rhapsodies. "Your bosoms, your shoulders and hips are round, your waist is tiny, your skirt's bulk suggests fragile feminine legs," caroled their glossy pages. The skimpy wartime look had fallen, said "Vogue" and "Harper's Bazaar." In its place was Dior's full-flowered "New Look."

The quick switch promised a bundle of cash both to designers and manufacturers; and fashion editors were quick to push their advertisers' new product. "In this issue," purred "Vogue" in typically tipsy

phrasing, "the merits of the cautious discard." The sledgehammer directive: throw out everything and buy a whole new wardrobe. For the average woman (or her husband), this meant an outlay of from $20 to $450 per dress, depending on where she shopped.

American men were dismayed by the disappearance not only of their cash but also of their ladies' legs. And not all American women rejoiced at the style revolution. In Dallas, 1,300 women formed the Little Below the Knee Club. In Louisville 676 office girls signed a petition against the New Look. In New York City, Presidential envoy Mrs. Anna Rosenberg joined the fray: "It shows everything you want to hide and hides everything you want to show." Even Dior was dismayed at the furor he created. "My God, what have I done?" he murmured—en route to the bank.

1   2   3

252

The New Look in Arkansas

Three months after Dior presented a New Look creation at $450 in France, wholesale dress manufacturers in New York began cranking out copies like those shown here. Using rayon instead of silk, four elegant flounces instead of eight—and high-speed electric cutters—the mass-production geniuses sewed up a million dresses within weeks. Then, as fast as a garment-district schlock meister could say "100,000 yards of taffeta—by Thursday, Morris," any woman who wanted the look of Paris, France, could get it in Paris, Arkansas, for $20 or less.

Straight from Paris—via New York—are the gently sloping shoulders, the curving waist of a classic $19.95 suit dress in royal blue flannel (1). A $14.95 afternoon dress of blue and white tie silk has a neckline new for now—the deep, deep plunge (2). Slipping off the shoulders is the taffeta of a chic $17.95 cocktail dress (3). For evening hours, an ensemble for $16.90: a frothy white organdy blouse blossoms from its peg-top velveteen skirt (4).

4

A Military Note

In the first half of the '40s, American dressmakers, unable to copy the delicate couturiers of Paris, borrowed ideas from—of all people—the Allied war-uniform makers. Thus, by various startling mutations, clothing originally conceived out of functional field necessities became fads of high fashion. Anna Miller, for example, even managed to adapt the homely wool windbreaker of America's General "Ike" for ladies' evening wear (below).

The "Eisenhower jacket" becomes a crepe blouse with a drawstring waist (1). A copy of the British tank corps beret tops an American's daytime suit (2). A. U.S. Women's Army Corps cap goes glittery with sequins (3). Eagle's wings take two gowns "into the wild blue yonder" of evening (right).

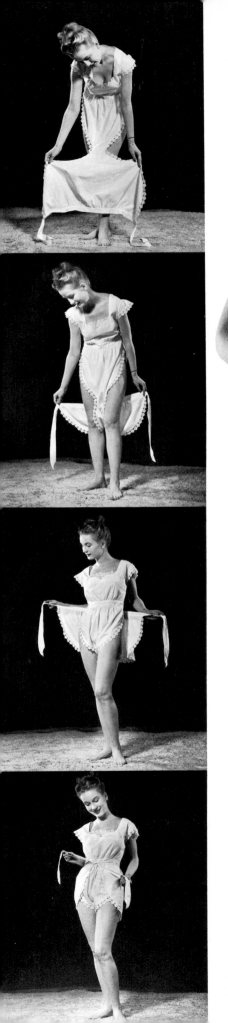

Skirting Regulations

During the '40s playclothes became a major fashion item, and fabric shortages in the war years encouraged the trend toward much simpler, scantier styles. For example, the Dido (left), a sort of grown-up romper suit, overcame government restrictions against extravagant ruffles, pleats and full-cut sleeves. Another order halted the production of zippers and metal fastenings; wraparound skirts met the challenge with a flare.

The war put a stop to full peasant skirts because each garment required three to five yards of fabric but a skimpier two-yard version came into fashion and was worn with peasant blouses (now shorn of their forbidden ruffles).

Donning the Dido, a model pulls the top part over her head, then draws the attached diaper through her legs and finally ties the sash around her waist. Made of cotton and costing a few dollars, the Dido served as both an abbreviated nightie and a playsuit.

Ready for a swim or a lawn party, the versatile
girl (at left) unwinds her wraparound skirt to reveal a bathing
suit. Stripes—vertical, horizontal and diagonal—were
a favored pattern, as evidenced also by the dirndl skirt below.

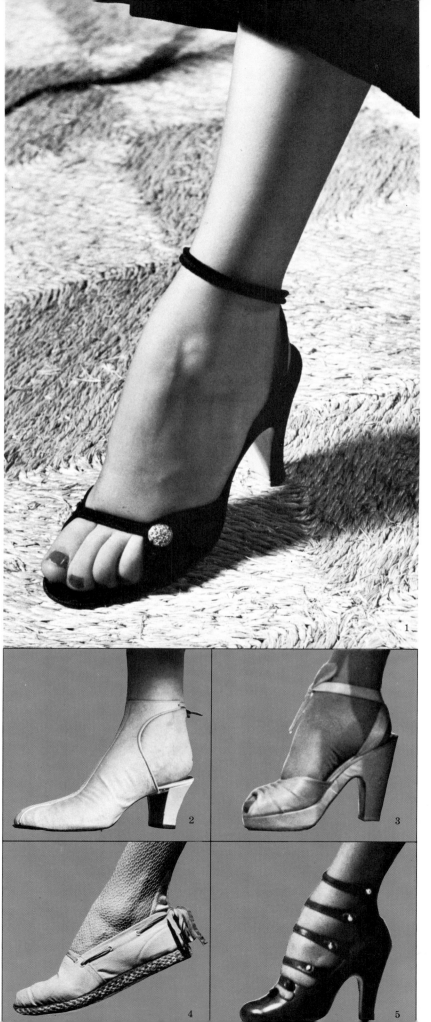

Accent on Accessories

No matter how perfect the line of her dress or the cut of her suit, the well-dressed woman of the '40s felt incomplete until she had added the right pair of gloves, or an eye-catching hat and purse. Once the New Look had taken hold, shoes were the accessories that took on supreme significance. Since the long skirts revealed only 12 inches of calf, women with good legs had to resort to extreme measures (left) to draw attention to their assets; high heels and bizarre ankle straps were some of the devices that accomplished the task.

The spike-heeled "Naked Sandal" (1) epitomized the "barefoot look." The backless linen boot (2) was a postwar playshoe; and the clunky platform (3) also hit it big in the late '40s. Espadrilles (4) were a peasant fad while multiple ankle straps (5), worn with colored nylons, enhanced the New Look.

A mania for matching broke out in 1944. That year, Hattie
Carnegie paired a fluted "abbess" hat with cuffed gloves
(1); another designer used fluted felt for a "skyscraper hat" and a
bag (2). A striped hat by John-Frederics found
a sharp echo in a handbag (3), while a parasol patterned like a
spider web (4) co-ordinated—dizzyingly—with a blouse.

Fads and Fantasies

The '40s were full of fads, some fostered by necessity, some by science and some by whimsy. Leg make-up was an ingenious alternative to rayon and cotton stockings. After the war, nylon gave birth to the wash-and-dry dress, a practical travel item ready to wear two hours after a scrubbing. A brief craze for beauty patches, however, owed its existence merely to an appetite for fantasy.

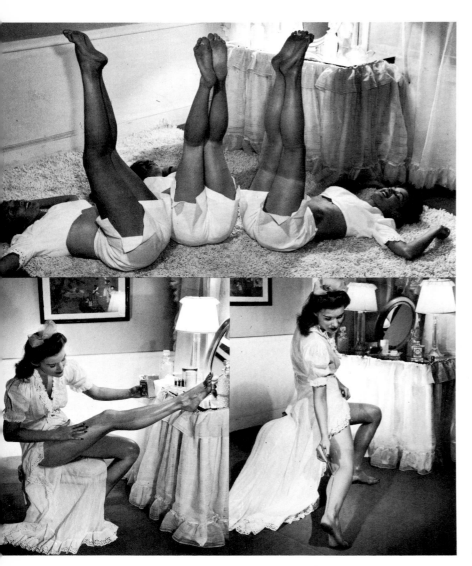

Beauty patches, adhesive bits of black silk cut in various shapes, accentuate the eyes, lips or back.

Wartime girls hoist their legs to show varied lengths of "bottled" stockings; fake seams are made with an eyebrow pencil.

The nylon dress, a boon to women on the go, regains its soft, billowy look with no ironing after hanging up to dry.

In 1947 photographs of everything from giant roses (below) to portraits of the wearer were printed on dress fabrics.

The strapless, wired bra, which came out in 1946, complements the new bare-shouldered look.

The Crowning Touch

The woman of the '40s seemed never to go anywhere without a hat. Whether she was shopping in the daytime or attending the theater at night, she almost invariably had something on her head. And almost invariably, it was nonsensical—a high turban or perhaps a wide sailor, festooned with a veil and generally sprouting a profusion of feathers, folds and pleats. The so-called "millinery creations" of the postwar years were often wildly expensive: for a sprightly headpiece many women thought nothing of laying down $60 to $70—sometimes more than they spent for the rest of their ensemble.

The extravagant femininity of women's fashions in the '40s was emphasized by hats with giant flowers (1). Rose Saphire's draped postilion soars eight inches above the brow (2). John-Frederics' blown-up derby is aptly named "Global" (3). And at right John-Frederics' chapeau sports half a barnyard of feathers.

Theater

Mary Martin struts onstage in "South Pacific."

Oh, What a Beautiful Era

I don't want realism. I want magic! Yes, yes, magic! I try to give that to people. I misrepresent things to them. I don't tell the truth, I tell what ought to be the truth. And if that is sinful, then let me be damned for it!

BLANCHE DU BOIS IN *A STREETCAR NAMED DESIRE*

The words above might well have been the rallying cry of postwar Broadway, as the theater ushered in its brightest epoch of musical comedy and straight drama. Gone were the self-conscious political plays of the '30s that had taken the country to task for its social inequities. Gone also were dramas about war and the evils of fascism. Enter: *Annie Get Your Gun, Carousel* and *Kiss Me, Kate,* among the longest-running and most-acclaimed musicals in history. Enter, too, Arthur Miller's *Death of a Salesman* and Tennessee Williams' *A Streetcar Named Desire,* plays that analyzed people, not politics.

Broadway had to battle for this new success in a highly unfavorable climate. Never had it been more difficult to mount a production. In the '20s a lavish show had cost under $100,000; after the war, many musicals required as much as $250,000 to produce. In the season of 1928-1929 Broadway saw 200 productions; in 1949-1950, only 62 major productions appeared. Worse yet, there was a frightening rise in competition for the entertainment dollars. Television was beginning to steal audiences; sports, buoyed by the return of its prewar heroes *(pages 222-225),* also drew away the crowds. When sports and television joined forces, the effect was devastating; in 1947 the World Series was telecast for the first time and Broadway reported a 50 per cent slump in business.

In the face of such hazards, many showmen became conservative, scheduling revivals of tried-and-true successes or staging low-risk adaptations of popular novels. During the period of uncertainty, lightweight comedies —like *Harvey,* starring Frank Fay, and *Born Yesterday,* which made Judy Holliday famous—became the commercial mainstay of the ailing theater.

But happily, Broadway had a reservoir of new talent *(following pages)* to overcome its woes. In the final years of the decade, musical comedies were returning profits of as much as 500 per cent. And the artistic quality of the theater had risen markedly. On January 1, 1950, Broadway song writers Richard Rodgers and Oscar Hammerstein II proudly wrote in *The New York Times:* "We believe that our modern American theater is courageous, adventurous, not dying, in fact very much alive. We have two new remarkably talented playwrights—Tennessee Williams and Arthur Miller. Two talents of their caliber rarely rise in one decade. Two are a lot. As for the American light musical theater, it is beginning to be recognized in other parts of the world as the best of its kind today."

A 1945 drawing by Albert Hirschfeld pictures Laurette Taylor (top, right), with (clockwise) Frederic O'Neal, Judy Holliday and Frank Fay.

The Sour Smell of Success

The debut of playwright Tennessee Williams was thoroughly unpromising. His first major attempt, *Battle of Angels,* closed after a few days in Boston in 1941.

Following this debacle, Williams worked as a waiter, an elevator operator and finally as a Hollywood scriptwriter—from which post he was soon fired. While being sacked, he wrote a very melancholy play about a faded Southern belle, her crippled daughter and ne'er-do-well son. Called *The Glass Menagerie,* it opened in New York in 1945 and was a smashing success. Williams became so famous so fast that it nearly unbalanced him, as he related in the essay excerpted below, which appeared in *The New York Times* on November 30, 1947, four days before the opening of his next triumph, *A Streetcar Named Desire.*

Sometime this month I will observe the third anniversary of the Chicago opening of "The Glass Menagerie," an event which terminated one part of my life and began another about as different in all external circumstances as could be well imagined. I was snatched out of virtual oblivion and thrust into sudden prominence, and from the precarious tenancy of furnished rooms about the country I was removed to a suite in a first-class Manhattan hotel. My experience was not unique. Success has often come that abruptly into the lives of Americans.

The sort of life which I had had previous to this popular success was one that required endurance, a life of clawing and scratching along a sheer surface and holding on tight with raw fingers to every inch of rock higher than the one caught hold of before, but it was a good life because it was the sort of life for which the human organism is created.

I sat down and looked about me and was suddenly very depressed. I though to myself, this is just a period of adjustment. Tomorrow morning I will wake up in this first-class hotel suite above the discreet hum of an East Side boulevard and I will appreciate its elegance and luxuriate in its comforts and know that I have arrived at our American plan of Olympus. Tomorrow morning when I look at the green satin sofa I will fall in love with it. It is only temporarily that the green satin looks like slime on stagnant water.

I soon found myself becoming indifferent to people. A well of cynicism rose in me. Conversations all sounded like they had been recorded years ago and were being played back. Sincerity and kindliness seemed to have gone out of my friends' voices. I suspected them of hypocrisy. I stopped calling them, stopped seeing them. I was impatient of what I took to be inane flattery.

I got so sick of hearing people say, "I loved your play!" that I could not say thank you any more. I choked on the words and turned rudely away from the usually sincere person. I no longer felt any pride in the play itself but began to dislike it, probably because I felt too lifeless inside ever to create another. I was walking around dead in my shoes, and I knew it but there was no one I knew or trusted sufficiently, at that time, to take him aside and tell him what was the matter.

I checked out of the suite at the first-class hotel, packed my papers and a few incidental belongings and left for Mexico, an elemental country where you can quickly forget the false dignities and conceits imposed by success, a country where vagrants innocent as children curl up to sleep on the pavements and human voices, especially when their language is not familiar to the ear, are soft as birds'. My public self, that artifice of mirrors, did not exist here and so my natural being was resumed.

Then, as a final act of restoration, I settled for a while at Chapala to work on a play called "The Poker Night," which later became "A Streetcar Named Desire." It is only in his work that an artist can find reality and satisfaction, for the actual world is less intense than the world of his invention and consequently his life, without recourse to violent disorder, does not seem very substantial. The right condition for him is that in which his work is not only convenient but unavoidable.

One does not escape easily from the seductions of an effete way of life. You cannot arbitrarily say to yourself, I will now continue my life as it was before this thing. Success happened to me. But once you fully apprehend the vacuity of a life without struggle you are equipped with the basic means of salvation. Once you know this is true, that the heart of man, his body and his brain, are forged in a white-hot furnace for the purpose of conflict (the struggle of creation) and that with the conflict removed, not privation but luxury is the wolf at the door and the fangs of this wolf are all the little vanities and conceits and laxities Success is heir to—why, then with this knowledge you are at least in a position of knowing where danger lies.

The Glass Menagerie

Laurette Taylor as Amanda Wingfield dreams of the time when she
was young and had "seventeen gentlemen callers." In 1912 Miss Taylor became America's
darling when she starred in "Peg O' My Heart," but she had sunk into
obscurity before "The Glass Menagerie" opened. She died shortly after "Menagerie"
closed, but not before winning every award as top Broadway actress.

A Streetcar Named Desire

*Marlon Brando, playing the crude Stanley Kowalski in Williams' 1947
play, manhandles the sensitive and aristocratic Blanche Du Bois, acted by Jessica Tandy.
Brando was catapulted to fame by this role, but critic Harold Clurman
complained that Brando's own "introspective, and almost lyric personality" made the
character too sympathetic and threw the production out of focus.*

A Smile Gets You No Place

ARTHUR MILLER

At 8:15 on the morning of February 11, 1949, a double file of Broadway playgoers started to line up outside the box office of the Morosco Theater on West 45th Street. Before 10:00 the ticket queue choked the sidewalks all the way down the block to Eighth Avenue. The scramble was for tickets to Arthur Miller's *Death of a Salesman*, which had just opened the night before to smash reviews. The tumult would continue through the end of 1950, when the show finally closed after winning both the Pulitzer Prize and the Drama Critics' Circle Award.

The box-office success of *Death of a Salesman* was matched by the emotional wallop the play generated. At the final curtain of its pre-Broadway debut in Philadelphia, the audience refused to go home. For almost an hour after the play ended, people stood near their seats or milled around the theater lobby, reeling from the impact of an American tragedy about an average guy—a 63-year-old traveling salesman who was at the end of the road and the end of his rope.

Willy Loman, the central character of the drama, was somebody everybody seemed to recognize. He was a man who worshiped material success, believed it came entirely by "riding on a smile and a shoeshine"—and finally killed himself. He chose suicide because he realized that he was a complete failure and that his two dearly loved sons, whom he had reared with the same set of values, had turned out to be weaklings and total failures, too.

Most Americans who came to see the play seemed to have cousins, uncles and brothers in the same boat as Willy Loman. Lee J. Cobb, the actor who played Willy for 330 grueling performances, received some 40 or 50 letters a week from people who wanted to tell him about the Willys they knew. Mature women wrote objectively but often intimately about their lives with husbands like Willy. One woman said she never understood why her husband and sons fought so bitterly until she saw Willy Loman fighting on stage with his sons. Another became so involved with the play that she wrote: "I think I shall forevermore be allergic to the words 'pull yourself together.' When you stood so forlornly on the stage after that beast told you those words and you said, 'What did I say?' my heart rushed out to you, for you were a man that was bewildered and weary and I had all I could do not to rush on the stage and give you a helping hand."

There were stacks of letters from men, too, salesmen and others, many of whom recognized either themselves or their families all too clearly in Miller's shatteringly realistic play. However, there was a hardy handful of males who managed to miss the point altogether. Wrote one such to Cobb: "I was disgusted with your appearance. Don't you ever have your pants pressed? And why don't you go on a diet?" Perhaps the most uncomprehending —and funniest—remark of all was made by a salesman who said to another as they were leaving the theater, "Well, that New England territory always was tough."

Death of a Salesman

Lee J. Cobb as Willy Loman postures over his sons, Cameron Mitchell as Happy, left, and Arthur Kennedy as Biff. When Biff says he "borrowed" his new football from the school locker room, Willy laughs: "Coach'll probably congratulate you on your initiative."

The RH Factor

In the summer of 1942, Richard Rodgers was feeling terrible. Although the greatest hit of his career so far, *By Jupiter*, had just opened, his lyricist and collaborator of 25 years, Lorenz Hart, was depressed and ready to quit. Hart had always been eccentric, if brilliant; he had a habit of disappearing for days at a time when he was supposed to be working on a show.

During the work on *By Jupiter*, Hart had worried himself into such a state of nerves that he checked into a hospital. Rodgers promptly moved into a nearby room, bringing along a piano in hopes of squeezing some lyrics from his partner. Somehow the songs got written, but afterward Hart gave up altogether and headed to Mexico for a rest. The timing of his departure could hardly have been worse, for a production group called the Theatre Guild was about to ask Rodgers to compose a new musical based on an old play called *Green Grow the Lilacs*.

If Rodgers' life was difficult, Oscar Hammerstein's was downright miserable. More than a decade had gone by since his last big hit; and in the past four years, he had suffered three crushing Broadway disasters. Four of the movies for which he had written lyrics had been junked, while two that were released had flopped. A Hollywood executive declared: "He can't write his hat."

At this low point, Hammerstein received a call from Rodgers asking if he might want to try some lyrics for a musical version of *Lilacs*. By sheer coincidence, Hammerstein all on his own had become interested in the musical possibilities of the same play. He had even read it aloud to Jerome Kern, hoping to form a musical partnership on the show. But Kern had turned it down, saying the play's third act was weak. Hammerstein, however, was still convinced the play was promising, and he jumped at the chance of working on it with Rodgers.

Rodgers *(seated at right)* and Hammerstein *(standing)* worked perfectly together from the start. Unlike the mercurial Hart, Hammerstein was as punctual and efficient as a Wall Street executive. And his lyrics were superb. "The very first lyric that Oscar finished," Rodgers said, "was 'Oh, What a Beautiful Mornin',' and when he handed it to me and I read it for the first time I was a little sick with joy because it was so lovely and so right."

In their unruffled and masterful way, Rodgers and Hammerstein went on to turn *Green Grow the Lilacs* into a musical called *Oklahoma!* In quick succession, they followed with *Carousel* (1945) and *South Pacific* (1949). The list of songs from each show *(below)* reads much like a hit parade of the late '40s. From a peak of success never before reached by any Broadway musical partnership, Richard Rodgers offered a modest explanation: "What happened between Oscar and me was almost chemical. Put the right components together and an explosion takes place."

OKLAHOMA!	CAROUSEL	SOUTH PACIFIC
OH, WHAT A BEAUTIFUL MORNIN'	YOU'RE A QUEER ONE, JULIE JORDAN	DITES-MOI POURQUOI
THE SURREY WITH THE FRINGE ON TOP	WHEN I MARRY MR. SNOW	A COCKEYED OPTIMIST
KANSAS CITY	IF I LOVED YOU	SOME ENCHANTED EVENING
I CAIN'T SAY NO	JUNE IS BUSTIN' OUT ALL OVER	BLOODY MARY IS THE GIRL I LOVE
MANY A NEW DAY	WHEN THE CHILDREN ARE ASLEEP	THERE IS NOTHING LIKE A DAME
IT'S A SCANDAL! IT'S AN OUTRAGE!	BLOW HIGH, BLOW LOW	BALI HA'I
PEOPLE WILL SAY	SOLILOQUY	I'M GONNA WASH THAT MAN RIGHT OUTA MY HAIR
PORE JUD	THIS WAS A REAL NICE CLAM BAKE	I'M IN LOVE WITH A WONDERFUL GUY
LONELY ROOM	GERANIUMS IN THE WINDER	YOUNGER THAN SPRINGTIME
OUT OF MY DREAMS	THERE'S NOTHIN' SO BAD FOR A WOMAN	HAPPY TALK
THE FARMER AND THE COWMAN	WHAT'S THE USE OF WOND'RIN	HONEY BUN
ALL 'ER NOTHIN'	YOU'LL NEVER WALK ALONE	YOU'VE GOT TO BE TAUGHT
OKLAHOMA!	THE HIGHEST JUDGE OF ALL	THIS NEARLY WAS MINE

In the months before *Oklahoma!* arrived on Broadway, no show ever seemed less likely to succeed. The original play, *Green Grow the Lilacs,* had run for only 64 performances when it was first produced in 1931. For its musical re-incarnation, the director chosen was Rouben Mamoulian, who had worked on only one musical previously—and that had flopped. There were no stars, little racy humor and none of the splashy chorus-girl numbers that had always been considered the backbone of a Broadway musical.

Raising money for such an unlikely production was slow and agonizing. At auditions set up to lure backers, Rodgers played the score on the piano and Hammerstein narrated the plot. The results were dismal. At two auditions not a single dollar was raised (one guest commented he never did like plays about farmers). Those who did contribute money did so only as a favor to the Guild or to Rodgers and Hammerstein. But slowly the money dribbled in and the musical managed to get into rehearsal. Under the provisional title *Away We Go,* it opened in New Haven and one New York sharpie carried the verdict back to Broadway: "No Girls, No Gags, No Chance." Newly christened *Oklahoma!,* it next went to Boston, where some of the cast came down with measles and had to wear thick layers of makeup to hide their spots. When the production finally limped into New York, there were empty seats at the opening-night performance and the first public reaction came from a radio critic who predicted the show would not last a week.

The rest of New York thought otherwise. The most cautious commentary came from the *New York Herald Tribune,* which called it "a jubilant and enchanting musical." The

Oklahoma!

*A cowboy and his girl leap in one of the dances
by Agnes de Mille, a ballet choreographer. In its review, "Time"
said: "Even run-of-de-Mille dances have more style
and imaginativeness than most Broadway routines, while
the best are almost in a different world."*

New York World-Telegram proclaimed that Rodgers had written "one of the finest musical scores any musical play ever had," and LIFE declared flatly it was "Broadway's most enchanting show." The verdict of the sharpies was changed to: "No Girls, No Gags, No Tickets." When *Oklahoma!* finally closed in 1948, it had played 2,248 performances, a record for musicals. Within a few more years, each investor who had put $1,500 into the original kitty had already received back $50,000.

Oklahoma! turned the pickup partnership of Rodgers and Hammerstein into a major musical industry. The recordings from *Oklahoma!* (the first album ever to be made by the original cast of a Broadway show) sold over a million copies. While the royalties were still rolling in, the partners scored their second Broadway hit with *Carousel*. Meanwhile they set up their own production company to present other people's plays and musicals. Finally, in April 1949, they climaxed their collaboration with their own finest show, *South Pacific (left)*.

Based on novelist James A. Michener's book *Tales of the South Pacific*, Hammerstein's script set the musical story on an island in the Pacific during World War II. The plot told of the love of an American Navy nurse, Nellie Forbush, and a French planter, Émile de Becque. To play the part of De Becque, Rodgers and Hammerstein signed the Metropolitan Opera basso, Ezio Pinza, who sensed a turning point in his career and wanted to try a musical. Then they approached Mary Martin and asked her to play Nellie. Her spoken reaction was, "Why do you need two basses!"—a flippant reference to her own deep alto voice. But truthfully she was terrified at the idea of singing in du-

ets opposite Pinza, with his huge, trained, operatic voice.

"I've thought it out carefully, Mary," Rodgers reassured her. "You will never have to sing with Pinza in *opposition* to him. You'll sing in *contrast* to him." This was not just empty persuasion. For De Becque, Rodgers wrote powerful, romantic melodies—"Some Enchanted Evening" and "This Nearly Was Mine." Mary Martin's much thinner voice and Nellie's gee-whizzy personality were perfectly matched in "A Cockeyed Optimist" and "I'm in Love with a Wonderful Guy."

Mary Martin signed, the show went into rehearsal and the public's interest began to build. By the time the production opened in New York on April 7, 1949, the advance ticket sales totaled nearly a million dollars. The expectations were all justified. On opening night a correspondent for the London *Evening Standard* declared, "The only thing to do is take off one's hat, borrow an expressive old Americanism, and say 'Wow!'"

The success of Rodgers and Hammerstein in producing beautifully unified shows inspired other composers. Old-timers like Irving Berlin and Cole Porter—and the new team of Alan Jay Lerner and Frederick Loewe—abandoned the grab-bag way of doing musicals, emulated the new, integrated approach and, as a result, wrote three of the best shows ever: *Annie Get Your Gun; Kiss Me, Kate;* and *Brigadoon*. As Porter remarked, "The most profound change in forty years of musical comedy has been—Rodgers and Hammerstein." That change was indeed so profound that it helped make the '40s the most successful decade in the history of Broadway musicals. A sampling of scenes from these shows appears on the following pages.

South Pacific

Mary Martin, playing a Navy nurse dressed up for an amateur show, clowns with Seabee Luther Billis (Myron McCormick). For her role, Miss Martin had to stand under a shower eight shows a week to sing "I'm Gonna Wash That Man Right Outa My Hair."

Annie Get Your Gun

Playing sharpshooter Annie Oakley in Irving Berlin's
musical of 1946, Ethel Merman clutches her rifle and prepares to belt out a number.
Originally, the show's producers had asked Jerome Kern to do the songs. But
when Kern died Berlin took over, turning out such hits as "The Girl That I Marry,"
"Doin' What Comes Naturally" and "Anything You Can Do."

Kiss Me, Kate

*Patricia Morison bites a chunk out of Alfred Drake's hand as
they battle through a scene from the 1948 musical about Shakespearean actors performing
"The Taming of the Shrew." Set to the music of Cole Porter, the show
ran for 1,077 performances and included some of the best songs of Porter's career—
among them "Wunderbar," "Too Darn Hot," and "So in Love Am I."*

Brigadoon

*Highlanders celebrate a wedding in a mythical Scottish town
that appears for a single day every hundred years. With songs by Frederick Loewe and
Alan Jay Lerner, and choreography by Agnes de Mille, "Brigadoon"
won the Drama Critics' Circle Award for the best musical show of 1947; the score included
"Almost Like Being in Love" and "Come to Me, Bend to Me."*

Text Credits

36—"Juke Box Saturday Night" by Al Stillman & Paul McGrane, Copyright ©
1942 by Chappell & Co., Inc. Used by permission of Chappell & Co., Inc. 75
—Quote from *The Island War* by Major Frank O. Hough, J.B. Lippincott, Co., 1947,
p. 168. 77—Quote from *Yank: The GI Story of the War*, Duell, Sloan & Pearce, 1947,
p. 60. 78-79—Copyright © 1948 by Norman Mailer. Reprinted by permission of
the author and his agents, Scott Meredith Literary Agency, Inc. 85—Radio messages from *Carrier War* by Lieutenant Oliver Jensen, Pocket Books Inc., 1945, p.
83. 86—From *History in the Writing*, Gordon Carroll, ed., Copyright 1945 by Time
Inc., p. 83. 90—Quotes from "Raid on Regensburg" in *Combat: European Theater
World War II*, Don Congdon, ed., Dell Publishing Co., 1958, pp. 88, 101. 92—Adapt-
ed from *Once There Was a War* by John Steinbeck, Copyright 1943 by John
Steinbeck. Reprinted by permission of The Viking Press, Inc. 99—D-Day quotes
from *Yank: The GI Story of the War*, Duell, Sloan & Pearce, 1947, pp. 54, 91-93. 100
—From "On The Road to Berlin" from *Brave Men* by Ernie Pyle, Copyright 1943,
1944 by Scripps-Howard Newspaper Alliance and Holt, Rinehart and Winston,
Inc. Reprinted by permission of Holt, Rinehart and Winston, Inc. 102—McAuliffe
quote from *The Men of Bastogne* by Fred MacKenzie, David McKay Co., 1968, p.

217. 105—Quote from *Yank: The GI Story of the War*, Duell, Sloan & Pearce, 1947,
p. 12. 108—Reprinted by permission of HAROLD OBER ASSOCIATES INCOR-
PORATED, Copyright © 1943 by Paul Gallico. 110—Reprinted by permission of
HAROLD OBER ASSOCIATES INCORPORATED, Copyright © 1943 by Paul
Gallico. 112—Reprinted by permission of HAROLD OBER ASSOCIATES IN-
CORPORATED, Copyright © 1944 by Paul Gallico. 114—Reprinted by permis-
sion of HAROLD OBER ASSOCIATES INCORPORATED, Copyright © 1943
by Paul Gallico. 136—From *Up Front* by Bill Mauldin, The World Publishing Com-
pany, 1945. 174—Courtesy David J. Sheppard, Farmingdale, New York. 176
—From *A Book of Facts about the WAC*, Department of the Army, 1944. 213
—"NATURE BOY" by Eden Ahbez, Copyright © 1948 by Crestview Music Corp.
By permission of Ivan Mogull Music Corporation, New York, N.Y. 219—"It's
Howdy Doody Time" © 1950, Living Music, Inc. 220—Jingle reproduced with permission of PepsiCo Inc. 238—Copyright Newsweek, Inc., 1950. 240—Courtesy
SPORT Magazine Copyright © 1948, Macfadden-Bartell Corp. 268—Reprinted
by permission of The New York Times Company and the author. Copyright ©
1947 by The New York Times Company.

Picture Credits

*The sources for the illustrations in this book appear below. Credits for pictures from left to right are sep-
arated by semicolons, from top to bottom by dashes.*

Fabric design by John R. Martinez.
6,7—Courtesy Tommy Giles, Montgomery, Alabama. 8,9—Travel and Promotion
Division, Dept. of Conservation & Development, Raleigh, North Carolina. 10
through 13—Alfred Eisenstaedt from PIX, Inc. 14,15—Vernon T. Manion courtesy
Boeing Aircraft Company. 16,17—*Galveston Daily News*. 18,19—Library of Congress. 20,23—Culver Pictures. 24—"Umbrella Road," 1940 Herblock copyright cartoon for NEA Service. 26,27—Gordon Coster. 29—Nina Leen from PIX, Inc. 30,31
—Otto Hagel; Alfred Eisenstaedt from PIX, Inc.—Dale Stedman; Lisa Larsen.
32—Gordon Coster. 33—Nina Leen from PIX, Inc. 34,35—Nina Leen from PIX,
Inc.; Walter Sanders from Black Star; Marie Hansen. 36—Photo Files. 37—Bob
Landry. 38—Nina Leen from PIX, Inc. 39—Francis Miller; Gordon Coster—Edward Clark—Bernard Hoffman; Nina Leen from PIX, Inc. 40,41—Alfred Eisen-
staedt from PIX, Inc.; Peter Stackpole (2)—Edward Clark; Ralph Morse from
PIX, Inc.—Nina Leen from PIX, Inc. except center W. Eugene Smith from Black
Star. 42,43—Edward Clark. 44,45—United Press International; Hy Peskin; Cul-
ver Pictures; Johnny Florea; Culver Pictures; Johnny Florea—Wide World; From
Lincoln His Life in Photographs by Stefan Lorant, Duell, Sloan and Pearce; United Press International (3); Pictorial Publishing Co. 46—Edmund B. Gerard. 50,51
—All United Press International except top left Wide World and top right Culver
Pictures. 52,53—Edward Clark. 55—Drawing by Helen E. Hokinson; copr. ©
1945, The New Yorker Magazine, Inc. 56 through 61—Edward Clark. 62,63—Drawing by Helen E. Hokinson; copr. © 1942 The New Yorker Magazine, Inc. 64,65—Of-
ficial United States Navy photograph. 67—Wide World. 69—Official United States
Navy photograph. 73—Tsuguichi Koyanagi. 74—George Strock. 75—W. Eugene
Smith. 76,77—United States Army Signal Corps photograph; W. Eugene Smith.
80,81—J.R. Eyerman. 82,83—United Press International. 84,85—Official United
States Navy photograph. 87—Official United States Coast Guard photograph. 88,
89,90—Toni Frissell. 91—Official Photograph United States Army Air Force. 93
—Toni Frissell. 94,95—Wide World. 96,97—United States Army photograph. 98,99
—United States Coast Guard photograph. 101—Robert Capa. 102,103—Robert
Capa; United States Army photograph. 104,105—William Vandivert. 106,107,
Gatefold—Courtesy of the Philadelphia Quartermaster Corps. 108—Official Pho-
tograph United States Marine Corps. 109 through 115—All reprinted by permis-
sion of *Esquire Magazine* © 1943, 1943, 1944, 1943 by Esquire, Inc. 116—Wide
World. 118,119—All A.Y. Owen except second from left on bottom Eddy Van
der Veen, and second and third from right in center Henry Beville. 121—George
Silk. 122,123—Dmitri Kessel. 124—Photo Files. 125—R.R. Stuart Collection. 126
—Ralph Morse. 127—Culver Pictures. 128—Toni Frissell. 129—George Strock.
130—George Peck. 132,133—Ralph Morse (2)—United States Army Signal Corps
photograph; David E. Scherman. 134—Robert Capa. 135—Frank Scherschel.
136—John Phillips. 137—Copyright © 1944 Bill Mauldin. Reproduced by courtesy of Bill Mauldin. 138—Copyright © 1944 except lower right
Copyright © 1945 Bill Mauldin. Reproduced by courtesy Bill Mauldin. 139—

Copyright © 1944 except lower right Copyright © 1945 Bill Mauldin. Reproduced
by courtesy of Bill Mauldin. 140,141—Library of Congress. 143—*San Francisco
Chronicle*, May 6, 1944. 147—Herb Orth courtesy Charles Stillman—Henry B. Be-
ville courtesy Library of Congress. 148—Detroit Historical Museum;Margaret
Bourke-White. 150—Charles Phelps Cushing. 151—William Vandivert. 152,153
—Philip Gendreau. 155—Herb Orth courtesy United States Infantry Museum,
Fort Benning, Georgia—Sy Seidman—Henry B. Beville courtesy Library of Congress. 156,157—Culver Pictures; Eric Schaal. 158—The Collections of the Michigan Historical Commission; Wide World. 160—Fritz Goro. 161—*Philadelphia
Inquirer;* American Red Cross—Myron Davis. 162—All Library of Congress except center left *The Detroit News*. 163—State Department of Archives and History,
Raleigh, N.C. Print by North Carolina Museum of History; John W. Lewis—Library of Congress. 164,165—Culver Pictures—Detroit Historical Museum; Library
of Congress. 166—Library of Congress. 167—Dmitri Kessel. 169—Henry B. Beville courtesy Library of Congress. 170,171—© 1944, George Baker—Victor Barron.
172—United Press International; Library of Congress—Library of Congress; Wide
World—© 1944, George Baker. 173—George Strock. 174—United States Infantry
Museum, Fort Benning, Georgia—United States Army Signal Corps photograph.
175—United States Army photograph; Library of Congress—© 1944, George Baker. 176—Marie Hansen. 177—United States Marine Corps photograph; Marie Hansen—© 1946, George Baker. 178—© 1944, George Baker. 179—Peter Stackpole.
181—*The Saturday Evening Post*, May 29, 1943, courtesy of The Curtis Publishing
Co.—© National Periodical Publications, Inc. 1945. 182—© McNaught Syndicate,
Inc., Ham Fisher—Tony Dipreta. 183—All Gordon Campbell Collection except
bottom Paulus Leeser courtesy © 1942 by News Syndicate Co. Inc. 184—Culver
Pictures. 185—Metro-Goldwyn-Mayer, Inc. (2)—Edward Henderson for Paramount; Warner Bros. 186,187—All *The Saturday Evening Post*, Nov. 29, 1941; Feb. 7,
1942; April 11, 1942; Sept. 5, 1942; Jan. 1, 1944; Sept. 16, 1944; May 26, 1945; courtesy of The Curtis Publishing Co. Top two on right courtesy Culver Pictures. 188,
189—Sy Seidman, Photo Files, Culver Pictures. 190—Drawing by Chas. Addams;
Copr. © 1942, The New Yorker Magazine, Inc. 191—Reprinted by permission of *Esquire Magazine* © 1943 by Esquire, Inc.; Drawing by Alice Harvey; copr. © 1942,
The New Yorker Magazine, Inc.—Reprinted by permission of *Esquire Magazine*
© 1944; © 1944 by Esquire, Inc. 192—All reprinted by permission of *Esquire Mag-
azine* © 1944; © 1944— © 1944; © 1943 by Esquire, Inc. 193—Reprinted by
permission of *Esquire Magazine* © 1943 by Esquire, Inc. 195—Herb Orth courtesy
Charles Stillman except left Carter Smith. 196—Official Photograph, United
States Army Air Force courtesy Sam R. Quincey. 197—William Vandivert. 199
—All courtesy Federal Bureau of Investigation except top and lower left United
Press International. 200—Carl Iwasaki. 202—Library of Congress. 204,205
—Drawings from *Citizen 13660* courtesy of author, Miné Okubo. 207—Hansel
Mieth. 208,209—George Lyons courtesy of *The Boston Globe*. 210—Alfred Eisen-
staedt from PIX, Inc. 212—Nina Leen from PIX, Inc.; Matt Greene; United Press

International—Culver Pictures—no credit; Fritz Goro. 213—N.R. Farbman; "Don't Mind Me—Just Go On Talking," from *The Herblock Book* (Beacon Press 1952)—Peter Stackpole; Culver Pictures. 214—*Los Angeles Herald-Examiner* photo from International News photo; Allan Grant—Leonard McCombe; George Skadding. 215—Bob Landry; Jack Birns from Graphic House, Inc.; Leo Rosenthal from PIX, Inc.—Ralph Crane; Bernard Hoffman; Ralph Morse. 216—Paramount Pictures; Jim Whitmore—Albert Fenn—no credit; Martha Holmes. 217—*St. Louis Post-Dispatch*, November 9, 1945; Gordon Coster—Cornell Capa—Eric Schaal —George Karger from PIX, Inc. 218—Francis Miller; Jesse E. Hartman—Edmund B. Gerard; Alfred Eisenstaedt from PIX, Inc.—*St. Louis Post-Dispatch*, June 28, 1946. 219—NBC; no credit—Phil Stern from *Ebony;* Walter B. Lane—Walter Sanders; George Karger from PIX, Inc. 220—Jack Manning from PIX, Inc.; Peter Stackpole—Albert Fenn; Irving Hamberger. 221—Jean O. Reinecke; Yale Joel—Loomis Dean; H.G. Walker; Lisa Larsen. 222,223—New York *Daily News.* 225—W. Eugene Smith from Black Star. 226—United Press International—Wide World; New York *Daily News.* 227—United Press International (2)—*Philadelphia Inquirer.* 228, 229—Culver Pictures. 231—George Silk. 232,233—Hy Peskin. 234,235—Fred Bottomer. 236—Hy Peskin. 237—United Press International. 239—Ralph Morse.

240—Allan Grant. 241—United Press International. 242,243—George Skadding. 244,245—Nelson Morris. 246,247—Photograph by Irving Penn. Copyright © 1947 The Condé Nast Publications, Inc. 249—Copyright © 1947 by the Condé Nast Publications, Inc.—Cover by courtesy of *Harper's Bazaar*—Copyright © 1947 by the Condé Nast Publications, Inc. 250—Drawing by R.R. Bouché Copyright © 1949 by the Condé Nast Publications, Inc. 251—Thomas D. McAvoy. 252,253—Martha Holmes. 254—© Philippe Halsman. 255—Eileen Darby from Graphic House, Inc. 256—© Philippe Halsman. 257—Eileen Darby from Graphic House, Inc.; Nina Leen from PIX, Inc. 258—Nina Leen—Cornell Capa; Graphic House, Inc.—Peter Stackpole; Nina Leen. 259—All Nina Leen from PIX, Inc. except right © Philippe Halsman. 260—© Philippe Halsman. 261—Sharland from Black Star—Nina Leen. 262—Ralph Crane—Sy Seidman; © Philippe Halsman. 263—© Philippe Halsman. 264,265—W. Eugene Smith. 267—Courtesy of Al Hirshfeld from *The American Theatre As Seen By Hirshfeld.* 269—W. Eugene Smith. 270—George Karger from PIX, Inc. 271—Ron D'Asaro courtesy of Museum of the City of New York. 272—no credit. 273—W. Eugene Smith. 275—George Karger from PIX, Inc. 276,277—Gjon Mili. 278—W. Eugene Smith. 280—Eileen Darby from Graphic House, Inc. 281—Ralph Morse. 282,283—Gjon Mili.

Bibliography

Allen, Frederick Lewis, *The Big Change, 1900-1950.* Bantam Books, 1965.
Becker, Stephen, *Comic Art in America.* Simon & Schuster, 1959.
Biddle, Francis, *In Brief Authority.* Doubleday & Co., 1962.
Blum, Daniel, *A Pictorial History of the American Theatre.* Greenberg: Publisher, 1951.
Burns, James MacGregor, *Roosevelt: The Lion and the Fox.* Harcourt, Brace and World, Inc., 1956.
Carlson, John Roy, *Under Cover.* E. P. Dutton & Co., Inc., 1943.
Ewen, David, *Complete Book of the American Musical Theater.* Henry Holt and Co., 1958.
Farago, Ladislas, *The Broken Seal.* Random House, 1967.
Goldman, Eric F., *The Crucial Decade: America 1945-1960.* Random House, 1960.
Goodman, Jack, ed., *While You Were Gone.* Simon & Schuster, 1946.
Green, Abel, and Joe Laurie Jr., *Show Biz.* Henry Holt and Co., 1951.
Higham, Charles, and Joel Greenberg, *Hollywood in the Forties.* A. S. Barnes & Co., 1968.
Hoehling, A. A.:
   Home Front, U.S.A. Thomas Y. Crowell Co., 1966.
   The Week Before Pearl Harbor. W. W. Norton & Company, 1963.

Hough, Major Frank O., *The Island War.* J. B. Lippincott Co., 1947.
Lord, Walter, *Day of Infamy.* Holt, Rinehart and Winston, 1957.
Martin, Ralph, *The G.I. War.* Little, Brown & Co., 1967.
McWilliams, Carey, *Prejudice, Japanese-Americans: Symbol of Racial Intolerance.* Little, Brown & Co., 1944.
Millis, Walter, *This Is Pearl!* William Morrow & Co., 1947.
Morgenstern, George, *Pearl Harbor.* The Devin-Adair Co., 1947.
Myers, Debs, Jonathan Kilbourn and Richard Harrity, eds., *Yank—The G.I. Story of the War.* Duell, Sloan & Pearce, 1947.
Nelson, Benjamin, *Tennessee Williams. The Man and His Work.* Ivan Obolensky, Inc., 1961.
Prideaux, Tom, *World Theatre in Pictures.* Greenberg: Publisher, 1953.
Rodgers and Hammerstein Fact Book. Richard Rodgers & Oscar Hammerstein II, 1955.
Shaw, Arnold, *Sinatra.* Holt, Rinehart and Winston, 1968.
Smith, Bradford, *Americans from Japan.* J. B. Lippincott Co., 1948.
Toland, John, *But Not in Shame.* Random House, 1961.
Whitehead, Don, *The FBI Story.* Random House, 1956.
Wohlstetter, Roberta, *Pearl Harbor, Warning and Decision.* Stanford University Press, 1962.

Acknowledgments

The editors of this book wish to thank the following persons and institutions for their assistance:

Joseph Avery, Archives, Washington National Record Center; Dany Barker, New Orleans; Paul Bonner, The Condé Nast Publications, Inc., New York City; Sarah Boynton, LIFE Picture Collection, New York City; Mrs. Ruth P. Braun, Chief Librarian, *The Detroit News;* Burton Historical Collection, The Detroit Public Library; Greg Carpenter, Photographer, *Orlando Sentinel,* Orlando, Florida; Romeo Carraro, Head Librarian, *The Los Angeles Times;* The Honorable Richard H. Cooper, Orlando, Florida; Jim Coughlin, Orlando, Florida; Virginia Daiker, Prints and Photographs Division, Library of Congress; James H. Davis, Western History Division, Denver Public Library; Frank Driggs, New York City; Eugene Ferrara, New York *Daily News;* Sue Flanagan, Institute of Texan Cultures at San Antonio; Hugh R. Foley, Principal, Hollywood High School, Hollywood, California; Tommy Giles, Montgomery, Alabama; Leonard Huber, New Orleans; Mrs. Joye Jordan, North Carolina Museum of History, Raleigh; Frank Kavaler, The Curtis Publishing Co., Philadelphia; Labor History Archives, Wayne State University, Detroit; John W. Lewis Jr., Lafayette, Louisiana; William H. McDonald, Editor, *The Montgomery Advertiser,* Montgomery, Alabama; Mrs. Maier, Archives, Louisiana State University Library, Baton Rouge; Dr. William Mason, History Division, Los Angeles County Museum of Natural History; Bill Matthews, City of Miami Beach News Bureau; Michigan Historical Commission Archives, Lansing; Jane Milligan, The Saturday Evening Post Co., New York City; Joseph Molloy, Librarian, *The Philadelphia Inquirer;* Allen Morris, Florida State University, Tallahassee; Mrs. Grace Mullins, *The Galveston Daily News;* Sol Novin, Culver Pictures, New York City; Melvin Parks, Museum of the City of New York; Margot P. Pearsall, Curator, Social History Division, Detroit Historical Museum; Mrs. M. R. Pirnie, Montgomery, Alabama; Winthrop Sears Jr., Associate Archivist, Ford Archives, Henry Ford Museum, Dearborn; Sy Seidman, New York City; Russell Shaw, *Corpus Christi Caller-Times;* Dorothy Shipp, Chief, Photo Negative Files, *Fort Worth Star Telegram;* Mildred Simpson, Librarian, Academy of Motion Picture Arts and Sciences, Los Angeles; Ray Stuart, R. R. Stuart Collection, Los Angeles; Mrs. Betty Sprigg, Audio-Visual Division, Department of Defense; Richard W. Taylor, Research Staff, Photo Library, United Press International, New York City; Lieutenant Colonel Douglas B. Tucker, Information Officer, U.S. Army Infantry Center, Fort Benning, Georgia; Jerome A. Waterman, Maas Brothers Department Store, Tampa; David Wilson, Pix Incorporated, New York City.

Index

Numbers in italics indicate an illustration of the subject mentioned.

A

Above Suspicion (movie), *185*
Adkins, Homer M., quoted, 204
Ahbez, Eden, *213*
Air Force (movie), *185*
Air spotter, *156-157*
Air warfare, 24, 88, *89-91*, 92, *93*, 108
Aircraft carriers, 80, *81-84*
Airplanes, 88, *91*; losses of, in attacks on Germany, 88; war production, *14-15*, 22, 88, 150, *152-153*
Aleutian Islands, *122-123*
All-American Football Conference, 224, 234
Allen, Fred, 216
America First Committee, 22, 25
American People, Gorer, 54
Andrews, Dana, *184*
Annie Get Your Gun, 226, 279, *280*
Anson, Austin E., quoted, 203
Appliances, boom in, 221
Arm patches, military, *106-107*
Arms build-up, 142, 146, *147-153*; prewar, 22, 25. *See also* War production
Army Cook, The, quoted, 127
Army-Navy "E" pennant, *148*
Atlantic Ocean, 22, 86, *196*, 197
Austin, Warren, *219*
Axis powers, 22

B

B-17 bombers, *14-15*
Baby boom, 217
Baker, George, *Sad Sack* cartoons of, *170*, *172*, *175*, *177*, *178*
Baker, Wee Bonnie, 21
Baseball, 224, *225-233*; during war, 224, *226-227*; first Negroes in major leagues, 230, *231-233*; first telecast of World Series, 266
Bastogne, siege of, 102, *103*
Bataan, surrender at, *73*
Battle of Angels, Williams, 268
Battle of Britain, 24, 25
Battleships, eclipsed by carriers, 80
Beach: fashions, *257*; party, *40-41*
Beauty contest, *16-17*
Belgium, German invasion of, 22
Berg, Gertrude, *217*
Berle, Milton, *213*
Berlin, Irving, 279, *280*
Best Years of Our Lives, The, *212*
Bestsellers of 1945-1946, 213
Biddle, Francis, 194
Bilbo, Theodore, *219*
Births, 1942-1950, 217
Bombs, production figure, 150
Borah, William E., quoted 21
Borie, U.S.S., 86
Born Yesterday (play), 266
Borneo, 72
Boxing, *222-223*, 224, *236-237*, 238, *239*
Boyd, William, 215
Boys: teen-age, 28, *29*; conformity, 28, *31*, *34*; fashions, *34-35*; preoccupations of, 28, *36-43*
Bradley, Omar, 214
Brando, Marlon, *221*, *271*
Brigadoon (musical), 279, *282-283*
Broadway, drama and musicals, 264-283

Brooklyn Dodgers, 229, 230
Brown, Warren, quoted 224
Buna beach, *74*
Bunche, Ralph, *215*
Burger, Ernest, 198, *199*
Burke, Edward R., 22
Business: teen market, 28, 36, 37; wartime profits, 142
By Jupiter (musical), 274

C

Cahill, Ron, *226*
California, U.S.S., 71
Calship Yards, Los Angeles, *150*
Carlson, John Roy, 194
Carnegie, Hattie, 259
Carnera, Primo, 238
Carousel (musical), 266, 274, 279
Cars: new, *218*; used, 216
Cartoons: clubwomen, 54, *55*, *62-63*; F.D.R.'s 1940 candidacy, *23*; home front, *190-193*; Mauldin, 136, *137-139*; postwar, *213*, *217*, *218*; prewar, *20*, *24*; *Sad Sack*, 170, *172*, *175*, *177*, *178*
Casualties: air warfare, 88; island war, 72; Niseis, 206; at Pearl Harbor, 70
Censorship, GI mail, 130
Charles, Ezzard, 238
Chatfield, George, quoted, 48
Cherokee Indian reservation, *8-9*
Chevy Chase, Maryland, Woman's Club activities, 54, *56-61*
Chicago *Daily News*, 28
Chicago Tribune, 23
China, Japanese occupation of, 21, 66
Chrysler Arsenal, *151*
Churchill, Sir Winston, 25, 71, 146
Civil rights: Democratic plank of 1948, 212; Truman advocacy of, 220. *See also* Integration
Civilian Defense, 154, *155*, *156-157*
Clark, Chase, quoted, 204
Cleveland Browns, 234
Cleveland Indians, 224, 230
Clubwomen, *52-53*, 54, *55-63*
Clurman, Harold, quoted, 271
Cobb, Lee J., 272, *273*
Code, Japanese, broken by U.S., 68
Comics, wartime, *182-183*
Commercials, radio and TV, 216, 219, 220
Como, Perry, 50
Concentration camp, 131
Congress, war declaration vote, 25, 154
Congressional Medal of Honor, *118*; winners, *108-116*, 117
Conn, Billy, *222-223*, 224
Cooke, Alistair, quoted, 54
Coons, Hannibal, quoted, 240
Coral Sea, Battle of the, *82-83*
Corsair fighter planes, *152-153*
Cost of living, cartoon, *218*
Coughlin, Charles, 194
Crawford, Joan, *185*
Crosby, Bing, 47

D

Dance: musicals, *276-277*, *282-283*; teenagers, 36, *37*, *40*
Dasch, George, 198, *199*

Davies, A. Powell, quoted, 248
Day, Doris, *45*
D-Day, 94, *96-99*, 100, *101*
Dean, Dizzy, quoted, 230
Death of a Salesman, 266, 272, *273*
Decorations, military, *118-119*
De Mille, Agnes, 276, 283
Democratic National Conventions: of 1940, 23; of 1948, 212
Denmark, German invasion of, 22
Devereux, John, 71
Dewey, Thomas E., 216, 218
De Witt, John L., quoted, 201
Dido, *256*
Dietrich, Marlene, *133*; quoted, 49
DiMaggio, Joe, *44*, 224, *225*, 228
Dior, Christian, 248, *251*, 253
Displaced persons, immigration, *218*
Dixiecrat Party, 218
Dorsey, Tommy, 48
Draft: board, *10-11*, 170; bill, 22-23, 170; induction, *170-172*
Drake, Alfred, *281*
Drama, 266, 268, *270-271*, 272, *273*
Drive-in movie theaters, *214*
Drucker, Eugene P., 130; quoted, 131

E

Early, Steve, 71
Ebihara, Henry, quoted, 206
Eckstine, Billy, 50
Egg and I, The, MacDonald, 213
Eisenhower, Dwight D., 71, *96*, 97, *220*; quoted, 88, 97
"Eisenhower jacket," *254*
Employment: of veterans, 210; women, 54, 148
Eniwetok, 72
Enlistment, 168
Entertainment. *See* Broadway; Movies; Television; USO
"E" pennant, *148*
Espionage, 197
Esquire (magazine), 122; quoted, 108, 110, 112, 114; cartoons, 190, *191-193*
Europe, war in: air warfare, 24, 88, 90, *91*, 92, *93*; invasion of Normandy, 94, 97, *98-99*, 100, *101*; land warfare, 22, 94, *95-99*, 100, *101-105*, *110-111*; in 1940, 21, 22, 24

F

Falter, John, 108
Fashions, *246-247*, 248, *249-250*, 251, *252-263*; accessories, *258-259*; bare-shoulder look, *247*, *260-261*; beach, *257*; *Dido*, *256*; effect of war on, 248, 254, 256; hats, *259*, *262-263*; military look, *254-255*; New Look, 248, *250*, 251, *252-253*; shoes, 30, *31*, *215*, *258*; teenagers', *26-27*, 28, *30-31*, *34-35*
Fay, Frank, 266, *267*
Federated Women's Clubs, 54
Field hospital, *75*
"52-20 Club," 214
Fish, Hamilton, quoted, 25
Fisher, Ham, comics by, *182*
Fitzsimmons, Fred, *227*
Five Graves to Cairo (movie), *185*
Florida, saboteur landings, 198
Flying Fortress bomber, 88, *91*

Food: rationing, 142, 164, *166-167*; Sunday farming, 154, *158-159*
Football, 224, *234-235*; during war, *226-227*; Negroes in, 234, *235*
Foss, Joe, *108-109*
Foxx, Jimmie, *227*
France, 21; German defeat of, in 1940, 22; Normandy invasion, 94, 97, *98-99*, 100, *101*; GIs in, 131, *132-135*
Frazer, car, *218*
Fusari, Charley, *237*

G

Gallico, Paul, 108, 110, 112, 114
Gallup poll, August 1940, 23
Gardella, Danny, *227*
Gardner, Ava, 49-50, *215*
Gardner, Ed, *215*
Garfield, John, *185*
Garroway, Dave, *221*
Gasoline rationing, 142, 164, 165
Gavilan, Kid, *236*, 237
German-Americans, 194, 197
German saboteurs, 198, *199*
Germany: Allied strategy against, 94; bombing of, 88, 90, *91*; early war successes of, 21, 22; invasion of, *104-105*; U.S. war declaration against, 25
GI Bill of Rights, 210
GI life, 120, *121-129*, *132-139*; entertainment, *132-133*; equipment, *173*; fraternizing, *129*, 131, *134-135*; KP, *127*; leave and liberty, 178, *179*; letters on, 130-131; Mauldin cartoons, 136, *137-139*; pinup girls, *122-125*; *Sad Sack* cartoons, 170, *172*, *175*, *177*, *178*; training, *174-175*
Gilmore, Howard W., 114, *115*
Girls: teen-age, 28; conformity, 28, *30-31*; fashions, *26-27*, 28, *30-31*; preoccupations of, 28, *36-43*; Sinatra craze, *47-49*, *50-51*; slumber party, *32-33*
Glamour (magazine), fashions, 248, 249
Glass Menagerie, The, 268, *270*
Godfrey, Arthur, *216*
Goebbels, Joseph, quoted, 148
Goering, Hermann, 22
Goldbergs, The (serial), 217
Goldmark, Peter, *217*
Good Housekeeping (magazine), 210
Goodman, Benny, 210
Gorer, Geoffrey, quoted, 54
"Gorgeous George," *240-241*
Grable, Betty, 122, *125*
Graham, Billy, *221*
Graham, Otto, 234
Gray, Pete, *226*
Graziano, Rocky, 224, *237*
Great Britain, 21; German threat to, 22, 24; U.S. aid to, 22, 24-25
Green Grow the Lilacs (play), 274, 276
Growler, U.S.S., *114-115*
Guadalcanal, 72, 108, *126*
Guam, 72, 201

H

Hammerstein, Oscar II, 122, 274, *275*, 276, 279; quoted, 266
Harper's Bazaar (magazine): fashions, 248, *249*; quoted, 248

Harper's Magazine, 218
Harsch, Joseph, quoted, 71
Hart, Lorenz, 274
Harvey (play), 266
Hat fashions, *259, 262-263*
Haupt, Herbert, 198, *199*
Hayworth, Rita, 122, *124*
Heal, Edith, quoted, 30
Hearst newspapers, 49
Heinck, Heinrich, 198, *199*
Hendricks, Barbara, *219*
Hendrix, Wanda, 117
Henrich, Tommy, 228
Hersey, John, quoted, 86
Hirohito, Emperor, 66, 68
Hiss, Alger, 216
Hit songs, *36,* 213; Rodgers and
    Hammerstein, 274; Sinatra, 47, 48;
    wartime, *188-189*
Hitler, Adolf, 21, 22, 23, 24, 25, 148
Hobby, Oveta Culp, 176
Hokinson, Helen E., 54; cartoons by,
    55, 62-63
Holliday, Judy, 266, *267*
Home front, *140-141,* 142, *146-167;*
    arms production, 142, 146, *147-153;*
    cartoons, *190-193;* Civilian Defense,
    154, *155-157;* Japanese-Americans,
    200, 201, *202,* 203-206, *207;*
    rationing, 142, *164-167;* Red Cross
    volunteers, *160-161;* sabotage, 197,
    198; scrap collection, 154, *162-163;*
    shortages, 142, 146, *190, 191, 192;*
    spy scare, 194, *195,* 197, 201, 203
Home permanent, *212*
Hong Kong, 72, 201
Hope, Bob, 216
Hopkins, Harry, 68
"Hoppy" clothing, *215*
Hornet, U.S.S., *84,* 85
Hough, Frank O., quoted, 75
House Beautiful (magazine),
    quoted, 210
House I Live In, The (movie), 49
Household appliances, 221
Housing shortage, postwar, 210, *217*
Hucksters, The (movie), 215
Hull, Cordell, *67,* 68
Humphrey, Hubert H., *212*
Hutchins, Charles H., 86

I

Ickes, Harold, quoted, 23
Imamura, Akana, quoted, 206
Immigration: displaced persons, *218;*
    Japanese, prewar, 203
Indian reservation, *8-9*
Industry: fashion, 28, 248, 253; music,
    28, 36, 37; postwar conversion, 150.
    See also War production
Insignia, military, *106-107*
Integration: college, *219;* sports, 224,
    230, *231-235*
Irby, Edith Mae, *219*
Island war, 64-65, 72, *73-77,* 78-79
Isolationists, 21, 22, 23, 25
Issei, 203, 206. *See also*
    Japanese-Americans
Italy: Allied invasion of, 94;
    enters war, 22; U.S. war
    declaration on, 25
Iwo Jima, 72

J

Jacobs, Mike, 224
James, Harry, 48; quoted, 47
Japan: attack on Pearl Harbor, 25,
    66, 68, *69,* 70, 80; and China, 21,
    66; code broken by U.S., 68; prewar
    negotiations with, 66, *67,* 68; war
    preparedness, 66, 68
Japanese-Americans, 201-206; in
    armed forces, 206; evacuation of,
    194, *200,* 201, *202,* 203-204;
    internment of, *204-205,* 206, *207;*
    Issei, 203, 206; Nisei, 203, 206;
    prewar history of, 201-203;
    relocation of, 206; war contributions
    of, 201, 205, 206
Japanese fleet: in Battle of Midway,
    80; at Pearl Harbor, 68, 70
John-Frederics fashions, *259, 262-263*
Johnson, Hugh, quoted, 25
Journalism. *See* News reporting
Jukebox industry, 36

K

Kantor, MacKinlay, quoted, 142
Keep Your Powder Dry (movie), *185*
Kennedy, Arthur, *273*
Kennedy, John F., 71, *221*
Keppler, Reinhardt J., 112, *113*
Kerling, Edward, 198, *199*
Kern, Jerome, 274, 280
Kimmel, Husband E., 71, quoted, 68
Kinsey, Alfred C., *217*
Kiss Me, Kate (musical), 266, 279,
    281
Knox, Frank, quoted, 68, 70
Kurusu, Saburo, 66, *67,* 68
Kwajalein, 85

L

Ladies' Home Journal, 28, 210
Laine, Frankie, 50
Land warfare, 94, *95-99,* 100,
    101-105, 110-111
Lardner, John, quoted, 242
Lay, Beirne Jr., quoted, 90
Lend-Lease bill, 25
Lerner, Alan Jay, 149, 279, 283
Lexington, U.S.S., *82-83*
Lewis, Kathryn, 22
Liberator bomber, 88
Liberty Ships, 146
LIFE (magazine), 32, 44, 106, *218;*
    quoted, 47, 276
Lindbergh, Charles A., 22, 194
Lippmann, Walter, 201; quoted, 203
Living standard, 142
Loesser, Frank, 189
Loewe, Frederick, 279, 283
London, German bombing of, 24
London *Evening Standard,* quoted, 279
Long Island, saboteur landings, 198
Longworth, Alice Roosevelt, 22
Loo, Richard, *184*
Los Angeles Rams, 234
Louis, Joe, *222-223,* 224, 237, 238, *239*
LP (Long Playing record), invention
    of, 36, 217
Luciano, "Lucky," 49
Luftwaffe, 24, 88
Luxembourg, German invasion of, 22
Lynes, Russell, 218

M

MacArthur, Douglas, *45,* 70
McAuley, Ken, *227*
McAuliffe, Anthony, quoted, 102
McCormick, Myron, *278*
MacDonald, Betty, *213*
MacMurray, Fred, *185*
Magazines: fashion, *246-247,* 248, *249;*
    teen-age market, 28, 30; wartime
    covers and cartoons, 180, *181, 186-
    187, 190-191*
"Magic," 68, 70
Mahoney, Lee J., quoted, 122
Mailer, Norman, quoted, 78-79
Makin Island, *76-77*
Martin, Joe, quoted, 66
Martin, Mary, *264-265, 278,* 279
Mauldin, Bill, *136, 137-139*
Maxwell, Elsa, quoted, 48
Medals, *118-119*
Merman, Ethel, *280*
Metkovich, George, *226*
Michener, James A., 279
Midway, Battle of, 80
Military decorations, *118-119*
Military insignia, *106-107*
Military training, *174-175*
Miller, Anna, 254
Miller, Arthur, 266, *272;* quoted, 272
Miracle of the Bells (movie), 50
Mitchell, Cameron, *273*
Mitchell, Margaret, 21
Morgan, Henry, *219*
Morison, Patricia, *281*
Mortimer, Lee, 49
Motley, Marion, 234, *235*
Movies: drive-in, *214;* postwar, *212,*
    215, *216,* 220; Sinatra, 48, 49, 50;
    war, *184-185*
Murphy, Audie L., *116,* 117; medals
    of, *118-119*
Murray, Gerry, *242-243*
Murrow, Edward R., 24, 71
Music. *See* Hit songs
Music industry, 28, *36,* 37
Musial, Stan, 224
Musicals, *264-265,* 266, 274, *276-278,*
    279, *280-283;* production costs, 266

N

Naked and the Dead, The, Mailer, 78-79
National Football League, 224, 234
National income, 1940, 24
National Velvet (movie), 220
Nature Boy (song), 213
Naval warfare, 80, *81-85,* 86, *87,* 112-
    115. *See also* Submarine warfare
Negroes: enter major league sports,
    224, 230, *231-233;* first college
    integration case, *219*
Netherlands, German invasion of, 22
Netherlands Indies, 72
Neubauer, Hermann, 198, *199*
Neutrality acts, 21; broken, 22
New Guinea natives, *129*
New Look, 248, *250,* 251, *252-253*
New York *Daily Mirror,* 49
New York Herald Tribune, 48, 240, 267
New York *Star,* 50
New York Times, The, 22, 266, 268
New York World-Telegram, 279
New York Yankees, *228-229*

New Yorker, The, cartoons, *55, 190-191*
News reporting, 21-22, 24; war, 100,
    108, 142, *143-145*
Newsweek (magazine), quoted, 47, 238
Nimitz, Chester, quoted, 80
Nisei, 203; in armed forces, 206. *See
    also* Japanese-Americans
Nixon, Richard M., *216*
Nomura, Kichisaburo, 66, *67,* 68
Normandy, invasion of, 94, 97,
    98-99, 100, *101*
North Africa, Allied invasion of, 94
Norway, German invasion of, 22
Nuclear threat cartoon, *213*
Nye, Gerald, quoted, 71
Nylon, 260, *261*

O

Okinawa, 72, *77*
Oklahoma, U.S.S., 71
Oklahoma! (musical), 274, *276-277,* 279
Okubu, Miné: drawings of, *204-205;*
    quoted, 204
Omaha Beach, 98-99
O'Neal, Frederick, *267*
Outdoor life, *12-13, 18-19, 40-41*

P

Pacific Ocean: island war, *64-65,* 72,
    73-77, 78-79; naval warfare, 80, *81-
    85,* 112-115; U.S.-Japanese
    rivalry, 66
Paige, Leroy "Satchel," 230, *231;*
    quoted, 230
Paleface, The (movie), 216
Paratroopers, *94-95,* 102
Pasquel, Jorge, 224
Pearl Harbor, attack on, 25, 66, 68,
    69, 70-71; losses in, 70, 80
Peenemünde, Germany, *91*
Peg O' My Heart (play), 270
Penicillin, 212
Pep, Willie, 237
Philadelphia Phillies, *227*
Philippines: Japanese air attack on,
    70; surrender of, 72, *73,* 201
Phonograph records, 28, 36; LP, 36,
    217; Sinatra, 48
Pinups, GI, *122-125*
Pinza, Ezio, 279
Poland, German invasion of, 21
Porter, Cole, 279, 281; quoted, 279
Presidential elections: of 1940, 23-24;
    of 1948, *216,* 218
Prices: clothing, 251; hats, 262;
    meat, *166*
Progressive Party (1948), 218
Public opinion polls, 21, 22, 23
Purple Heart, The (movie), *184*
Pyle, Ernie, quoted, 100
Pyramid Clubs, 214

Q

Quirin, Richard, 198, *199*
Quonset hut, *122-123*

R

Race relations, 49, 219; civil rights
    champions, *212, 220;* college
    integration, *219;* Negroes in team
    sports, 224, 230, *231-235;*
    Nisei, 201-203

Radio, 24, *215*, 216, 217, *219, 220*
Rankin, Jeanette, 154
Rationing: food, 142, 164, *166-167;* gasoline, 142, 164, 165
Ratner, Payne, quoted, 204
Recruitment, 168, 170-172; posters, *169*
Red Cross, *128, 160-161;* poster, *181*
Reinecke, Jean O., 221
Republican convention of 1940, 23
Rickenbacker, Eddie, 108
Rickie, Branch, 230
Robinson, Jackie, 230, *232-233*
Robinson, Sugar Ray, *236*, 237
Rockwell, Norman, 180; *Saturday Evening Post* covers by, *181, 186-187*
Rodgers, Richard, 122, 274, *275*, 276, 279; quoted, 266, 274, 279
Rogers, Roy, *44*
Roller Derby, 240, *242-243*
Rommel, Erwin, 185
Roosevelt, Franklin D., *44*, 146, 182, 194, 198; and enemy aliens, 194, 201; quoted, 21, 22, 23, 24-25, 68, 71; third-term candidacy of, 21, *23*, 24; in U.S.-Japanese prewar crisis, 66, 68; and war in Europe, 21, 22, 24-25
Roper, Elmo, polls by, 21, 22
Rosenberg, Anna, quoted, 251
Rosie, the Riveter, 180, *181*
Ross, Murray G., quoted, 28
Rowe, Guy I., quoted, 174
Royall, Kenneth, 198
Ruark, Robert, quoted, 49
Russell, Harold, *212*
Ruth, Babe, *45*

S

Sabotage, 197; German attempts, 198
Saddler, Sandy, 237
St. Louis Cardinals, 230
Saipan, 72
Salsinger, H.G., quoted, 224
Saltonstall, Leverett, 163
San Francisco, U.S.S., 71, 112
Saphire, Rose, 262
Saturday Evening Post, The (magazine), 180; covers, *181, 186-187*
Savo Island, battle of, *112-113*
Schmeling, Max, 238
Scrap collection, 154, *162-163*
Sea warfare, 80, *81-85*, 86, *87, 112-115. See also* Submarine warfare
Selective Training and Service Bill, 22-23, 170
Seltzer, Leo, 242
Seventeen (magazine), 28
Sexual Behavior in the Human Male, Kinsey, 218
Sheridan, Ann, *131*
Sherman, Frederick C., quoted, 83

Sherman tank, 146
Shipping: British losses, 22, 24; off-shore sinking by U-boats, *196*, 197; U.S. war production, 146, *150*
Shoe fashions, 30, *31*, *215*, *258*
Sicily, Allied invasion of, 94, *110-111*
Sinatra, Frank, *46*, 47-50
Sinatra, Nancy B., 48, 49, 50
Singapore, 72, 201
Slumber party, *32-33*
Smith, "Cotton Ed," 163
Smith, Red, quoted, 240
"Snafu," 70
South Pacific (musical), 122, *264-265*, 274, *278*, 279
SPARS, 176
Sport (magazine), quoted, 240
Sporting News, The, 228
Sports, *222-223*, 224, *225-245*, 266; Negroes accepted in major leagues, 224, 230, *231-235*; professional, during war, 224, *226-227*; Roller Derby, 240, *242-243*; television's threat to live audiences, 224; TV quasi-sports programs, *240-243*; wrestling, 240, *244-245. See also* Baseball; Boxing, Football
Spy scare, 194, *195*, 197, 201
Stafford, Jo, quoted, 47
Stalin, Joseph, quoted, 146
Stark, Harold "Betty," quoted, 68, 70
Stars and Stripes (GI newspaper): Mauldin cartoons, 136, *137-139;* quoted, 49
State of the Union message, 1940, 22
Steinbeck, John, quoted, 92
Stengel, Casey, 228, *229;* quoted, 228
Stimson, Henry, 68, 176, 206
Streetcar Named Desire, A, Williams, 221, 266, 268, *271*
Stroheim, Erich von, *185*
Submarine warfare, 22, 86, 88, *114-115;* offshore, *196*, 197
Superman, 180, *181*
Sweeney, Martin L., 23

T

Taft, Robert A., *214;* quoted, 54
Tales of the South Pacific, 279
Tandy, Jessica, *271*
Tanks, production of, 146, 150, *151*
Tarawa, *64-65,* 72
Taylor, Elizabeth, *220*
Taylor, Laurette, *267, 270*
Teen-Age Manual, quoted, 30
Teen-age heroes, *44-45*
Teen-agers: business exploitation of, 28, 36, 37; conformity, 28, *30-31,* 33; dating, 30, *40;* revolution of, 28, *29-43. See also* Boys; Girls
Teheran Conference (1943), 146
Television, 210, *213, 215,* 217;

children's shows, 215, *219;* election reporting, *216;* sports programs, 224, *240-243,* 266; threat to other entertainment forms, 224, 266
Theater, *254-265,* 266, 268, *270-273, 274, 276-283;* cartoon, *267. See also* Broadway
Thiel, Werner, 198, *199*
Thomas, Norman, quoted, 24
Thurmond, Strom, 218
TIME magazine, 21; quoted, 66, 86, 142, 230, 276
To Hell and Back, Murphy, 117
Tojo, Hideki, 68
Trade embargo against Japan, 66
Trucks, war production, 150
Truman, Harry S, 198, 210, 214, *220;* re-election, *216,* 218
Tully, Grace, 71
Turner, Lana, *185*

U

U-boats, 86, 88, *196,* 197, 198
Ulithi, 72
"Ultras," 68
Undercover, Carlson, 194
Unemployment pay, veterans, 214
United Nations, 215, 219
University of Arkansas, *219*
U.S. Air Force, *87-91, 93*
U.S. Army: in Europe, *94-99,* 100, *101-105, 110-111;* and Nisei evacuation, 201, 204; at Pearl Harbor, 70; weakness in 1940, 22
U.S. Marines, *64-65*
U.S. Navy, *80-84,* 85-86, *87;* in Battle of Midway, 80; in Battle of the Coral Sea, *82-83;* battleships replaced by carriers, 80; at Pearl Harbor, 66, 68, *69,* 70-71, 80
USO entertainment, *132-133*

V

Vallee, Rudy, 47
Vandenberg, Arthur, *214*
Vera-Ellen, *44*
Victory cargo ships, *150*
Victory Gardens, 154, *158-159*
V-mail letter form, *130*
Vogue (magazine): fashions, *246-247,* 248, *249;* quoted, 248, 251

W

WACS, *176-177*
Wadsworth, James W., 22
Wainwright, Jonathan, quoted, 71
Wake Island, 72
Walker, Frank C., 122
Wallace, Henry, *218*
Wanted (movie), 215
War Bonds, 154; poster, *155*
War correspondents, 100, 108, 142

War in Boone City, The, Kantor, 142
War production, 22, 25, 142, 146, *147-153;* Army-Navy "E" pennant, *148;* labor, *147,* 148; materials, 163; planes, *14-15,* 22, 88, 150, *152-153;* quality, 146; share of gross national product, 146, 150; shipping, 146, *150;* statistics, *table* 150; tanks, 146, 150, *151*
War Relocation Authority, 204, 205, 206
War veterans, *208-209,* 210, *211, 212, 214*
Ward, U.S.S., 70
"Warmonger" charges, 22
WAVES, 176
Waybur, David, 110, *111*
Wheeler, Burton K., quoted, 23, 25
Wickard, Claude R., 158
Williams, Tennessee, 266, 268, *269*
Willie Gillis, 180, *186-187*
Willkie, Wendell, 23-24; quoted, 25
Women: clubs, *52-53,* 54, *55-63;* fashions, *246-247,* 248, *249-250,* 251, *252-263;* in the services, *176-177;* war efforts of, *160-163;* in war industry, *147-149;* wrestlers, *244-245*
Women Marines, 176, *177*
World War II: air warfare, 24, 88, *89-91,* 92, *93,* 108; called a Jewish-British plot, 22, 194; enlistment, 168; espionage, 197; island warfare, *64-65,* 72, *73-77,* 78-79; land warfare, 22, 94, *95-99,* 100, *101-105, 110-111;* 1940 events, 22, 24; Nisei combat records, 206; Pearl Harbor, 25, 66, 68, *69,* 70-71, 80; recruitment, 168, *169-172;* reportage, 100, 108, 142, *143-145;* sabotage, 197, 198; sea warfare, 80, *81-85,* 86, *87, 112-113;* submarine warfare, 22, 86, 88, *114-115, 196,* 197; U.S. arms build-up, 22, 25, 142, 146, *147-153 (see also* War production); U.S. entry into, 25, 154; U.S. forces, number of, 168; U.S. stance in early war, 21-25; U.S. unpreparedness, 66, 70, 71; women's services, *176-177. See also* Casualties; GI life; Home front
Wrestling, 240, *244-245*
Wylie, Philip, quoted, 54
Wyoming *State-Tribune,* quoted, 204

Y

Yank (GI newspaper), 77, 105, 130
Yasui, Kenny, 206
Your Hit Parade, 48, 50

Z

Zale, Tony, 224, 237
Zamperini, Louis, 221
Zoot suit, *35*